D1745940

OPRAH WINFREY
In Her Own Words

Raphael Afil

IN THEIR OWN WORDS SERIES

ISBN: 9782923241708

Copyright © 2021

www.raphaelafil.com

All rights reserved to Raphael Afil. No part of this book may be reproduced or transmitted in any form without the written permission of the author. Except for the inclusion of brief quotations in a review.

Biography	*5*
Stanford's Commencement ceremony	*10*
Wellesley Commencement Address	*27*
Harvard Commencement Speech	*38*
On Career, Life and Leadership	*52*
Speech at Power of Women	*84*
Keynote Speech at QuickBooks Connect	*94*
Harry's Last Lecture at Stanford University	*118*
Living Brave with Brene Brown	*140*
Empowerment Stage ESSENCE Festival	*152*
Agnes Scott Colleges 128th Commencement	*172*
USC Annenberg Class of 2018	*185*
Spellman Commencement Speech	*195*
Award for Lifetime Achievement at the Golden Globes	*200*
Goop Podcast with Gwyneth Paltrow	*204*
Speech at Women's E3 Summit at the Smithsonian	*252*
Powerful Eulogy for Toni Morrison	*280*
Graduation Class of 2020 Commencement Speech	*284*
Oprah Announcing the Coming End of her Show	*288*
Final Words on the last Oprah Winfrey's Show	*290*
Oprah Winfrey's Quotes	*291*

OPRAH WINFREY

Biography

Oprah Gail Winfrey was born in Kosciusko, Mississippi, on January 29, 1954. She was born as the result of what she called "a one-day fling under an oak tree" between her father and mother aged 18.

After spending her first six years on her grandmother's Mississippi farm, she moved to live with her single mother, who struggled on welfare in a poor Milwaukee, Wisconsin, neighborhood. Oprah battled a difficult childhood that included poverty, sexual abuse, and an early pregnancy that resulted in the premature death of the baby.

At 13 she was sent to Nashville to live with her father, who provided her with a secure life and education and had a positive influence in her life.

She was voted the most popular student at Nashville High School. Her public speaking and oratory skills were her most prominent skills. She won the beauty pageant Miss Black Tennessee at 17.

She won an oratory scholarship to Tennessee State University in 1971, and graduated with a Bachelor of Science degree in speech and drama.

At age 19 Winfrey became a news anchor for the local CBS television station. Following her graduation

OPRAH WINFREY

from Tennessee State University in 1976, she was made a reporter and coanchor for the ABC news affiliate in Baltimore.

She was not comfortable by the discipline and objectivity required for news reporting. In Baltimore in 1977, she became cohost of her first talk show; *People Are Talking*. The show became quite popular. Her outgoing and ardent personality started grabbing the public's attention.

Oprah excelled in the casual and personal talk-show format, and in 1984 she moved to Chicago to host the talk show *AM Chicago*. Her bright and engaging personality turned the program into a big success. Renamed in September 1985 as 'The Oprah Winfrey Show' the program started to broadcast on a national level. It became the highest-rated television talk show in the United States and earned several Emmy Awards.

At 30 years old, Oprah was competing with the veteran chat show icon Phil Donahue. Her show targeted various issues such as women's empowerment and human rights, addressing a broad mix of human issues, from family disputes to racism which appealed to people of all ethnicities and genders. Soon the whole of America was in love with this talented and magnetic personality who ran the show brilliantly.

In 1986 she created her own production company called 'Harpo' (her name spelled backwards). Harpo Productions Inc. gained the ownership and production rights to the Oprah

Winfrey Show from 1998 onwards. It produced other miniseries including 'The Women of Brewster Place' and movies like 'There Are No Children Here' (1993) and 'Before Women Had Wings' (1997).

Producer Quincy Jones spotted her on Chicago TV and asked Steven Spielberg to consider her for a role in *The Color Purple.* Her powerful acting debut brought her a best supporting actress Oscar nomination in 1986.

Her movies also include 'Charlotte's Web,' 'Bee movie' and 'The Princess and the Frog.' She has continued to act, including a role in the screen adaptation of Toni Morrison's *Beloved,* which she also produced.

In the early eighties, she met the love of her life, a PR executive with a graduate degree in education, Stedman Graham. They are still together but never married, when asked why they never tied the knot? She answered, "Once we settled we were going to be together, it ceased to be an issue. It just never comes up."

She co-founded a successful cable station called 'Oxygen' and changed the Discovery Health Channel to OWN: Oprah Winfrey Network that launched in January 2011.

Oprah published several self-help books, including *The Path Made Clear: Discovering Your Life's Direction and Purpose* (2019) and *What Happened to You? Conversations on Trauma, Resilience, and Healing* (2021; written with Bruce D. Perry).

OPRAH WINFREY

She publishes a magazine 'O, The Oprah Magazine.' Her website Oprah.com has an average of 70 million views and 6 million users every month. She signed a 55 million dollars contract with XM Satellite Radio to launch a new channel named 'Oprah Radio.'

Oprah Winfrey became the first black woman to make it onto the *Forbes* billionaire list, in 2003. She was already the most successful talk-show host in TV history and a producer, media mogul, actor, author and philanthropist of unparalleled cultural clout. In 2010 she was named a Kennedy Center honoree, and the following year she received the Jean Hersholt Humanitarian Award from the Academy of Motion Picture Arts and Sciences. In 2013 Winfrey was awarded the Presidential Medal of Freedom. She won the Cecil B. DeMille Award (a Golden Globe for lifetime achievement) in 2018,

A philanthropist who set up two charitable organizations Oprah's Angel Network and A Better Chance. In 2007 she opened a $40 million school for disadvantaged girls in South Africa. She donates at least ten percent of her massive income to good causes, mostly anonymously.

Oprah Winfrey and her longtime partner, Stedman Graham, never had any children together, but over the last 12 years, she's become "Mom O" to hundreds of girls.

In 2007, the Oprah Winfrey Leadership Academy for Girls (OWLAG) opened in South Africa, giving educational opportunities to bright, intelligent girls struggling with poverty in the area.

The inaugural class of 72 girls graduated in 2011, and have since gone on to achieve great things, like furthering their studies at such top universities like Harvard and Oxford.

The Charitable impact of the Oprah Winfrey's Charitable Foundation has as today donated more than 400 million dollars, educated 72,000 people and served more than 75 million meals.

She has been called one of the 'world's most powerful woman' by Time.com and CNN, Oprah has influenced the lives of millions of people and have made her as one of the most admired people of our time.

The goal of this book is to give exclusively to Oprah Winfrey, in her own words, to speak and explain what she thinks, what she wants and how she sees the future.

By listening to her speak and trying to explain her views and ideas, I discovered a woman with a sincere goal to contribute to make the world a better place. She is very intelligent, particularly sensitive to the spiritual forces that surround us. A firm believer in God, his mighty powers and love for each one of us, whatever our religion, color or beliefs. I learned a lot, you will also.

OPRAH WINFREY

Stanford's Commencement ceremony
(2008)

Thank you, President Hennessy, and to the trustees and the faculty, to all of the parents and grandparents, to you, the Stanford graduates. Thank you for letting me share this amazing day with you.

I need to begin by letting everyone in on a little secret. The secret is that Kirby Bumpus, Stanford Class of '08, is my goddaughter. So, I was thrilled when President Hennessy asked me to be your Commencement speaker, because this is the first time I've been allowed on campus since Kirby's been here.

You see, Kirby's a very smart girl. She wants people to get to know her on her own terms, she says. Not in terms of who she knows. So, she never wants anyone who's first meeting her to know that I know her and she knows me. So, when she first came to Stanford for new student orientation with her mom, I hear that they arrived and everybody was so welcoming, and somebody came up to Kirby and they said, "Ohmigod, that's Gayle King!" Because a lot of people know Gayle King as my BFF [best friend forever].

And so somebody comes up to Kirby, and they say, "Ohmigod, is that Gayle King?" And Kirby's like, "Uh-huh. She's my mom."

OPRAH WINFREY

And so the person says, "Ohmigod, does it mean, like, you know Oprah Winfrey?"

And Kirby says, "Sort of."

I said, "Sort of? You sort of know me?" Well, I have photographic proof. I have pictures which I can e-mail to you all of Kirby riding horsey with me on all fours. So, I more than sort-of know Kirby Bumpus. And I'm so happy to be here, just happy that I finally, after four years, get to see her room. There's really nowhere else I'd rather be, because I'm so proud of Kirby, who graduates today with two degrees, one in human bio and the other in psychology. Love you, Kirby Cakes! That's how well I know her, I can call her Cakes.

And so proud of her mother and father, who helped her get through this time, and her brother, Will. I really had nothing to do with her graduating from Stanford, but every time anybody's asked me in the past couple of weeks what I was doing, I would say, "I'm getting ready to go to Stanford."

I just love saying "Stanford." Because the truth is, I know I would have never gotten my degree at all, 'cause I didn't go to Stanford. I went to Tennessee State University. But I never would have gotten my diploma at all, because I was supposed to graduate back in 1975, but I was short one credit. And I figured, I'm just going to forget it, 'cause, you know, I'm not going to march with my class. Because by that point, I was already on television. I'd been in television since I was 19 and a sophomore. Granted, I was the only television anchor person that had an 11 o'clock curfew doing the 10 o'clock news.

Seriously, my dad was like, "Well, that news is over at 10:30. Be home by 11." But that didn't matter to me, because I was earning a living. I was on my way. So, I thought, I'm going to let this college thing go and I only had one credit short. But, my father, from that time on and for years after, was always on my case, because I did not graduate. He'd say, "Oprah Gail"—that's my middle name—"I don't know what you're gonna do without that degree." And I'd say, "But, Dad, I have my own television show."

And he'd say, "Well, I still don't know what you're going to do without that degree." And I'd say, "But, Dad, now I'm a talk show host." He'd say, "I don't know how you're going to get another job without that degree."

So, in 1987, Tennessee State University invited me back to speak at their commencement. By then, I had my own show, was nationally syndicated. I'd made a movie, had been nominated for an Oscar and founded my company, Harpo. I told them, I cannot come and give a speech unless I can earn one more credit, because my dad's still saying I'm not going to get anywhere without that degree.

So, I finished my coursework, I turned in my final paper and I got the degree. My dad was very proud. And I know that, if anything happens, that one credit will be my salvation.

But I also know why my dad was insisting on that diploma, because, as B. B. King put it, "The beautiful thing about learning is that nobody can take that away from you." And learning is really in the broadest sense what I want to talk about today, because your education, of course, isn't ending here. In many ways, it's only just begun.

The world has so many lessons to teach you. I consider the world, this Earth, to be like a school and our life the classrooms. And sometimes here in this Planet Earth school the lessons often come dressed up as detours or roadblocks. And sometimes as full-blown crises. And the secret I've learned to getting ahead is being open to the lessons, lessons from the grandest university of all, that is, the universe itself.

It's being able to walk through life eager and open to self-improvement and that which is going to best help you evolve, 'cause that's really why we're here, to evolve as human beings. To grow into more of ourselves, always moving to the next level of understanding, the next level of compassion and growth.

I think about one of the greatest compliments I've ever received: I interviewed with a reporter when I was first starting out in Chicago. And then many years later, I saw the same reporter. And she said to me, "You know what? You really haven't changed. You've just become more of yourself."

And that is really what we're all trying to do, become more of ourselves. And I believe that there's a lesson in almost everything that you do and every experience, and getting the lesson is how you move forward. It's how you enrich your spirit. And, trust me, I know that inner wisdom is more precious than wealth. The more you spend it, the more you gain.

So, today, I just want to share a few lessons—meaning three—that I've learned in my journey so far. And aren't you glad? Don't you hate it when somebody says, "I'm going to share a few," and it's 10 lessons later? And, you're like, "Listen, this is my graduation. This is not about you." So, it's only going to be three.

The three lessons that have had the greatest impact on my life have to do with feelings, with failure and with finding happiness.

A year after I left college, I was given the opportunity to co-anchor the 6 o'clock news in Baltimore, because the whole goal in the media at the time I was coming up was you try to move to larger markets. And Baltimore was a much larger market than Nashville. So, getting the 6 o'clock news co-anchor job at 22 was such a big deal. It felt like the biggest deal in the world at the time.

And I was so proud, because I was finally going to have my chance to be like Barbara Walters, which is who I had been trying to emulate since the start of my TV career. So, I was 22 years old, making $22,000 a year. And it's where I met my best friend, Gayle, who was an intern at the same TV station. Once we became friends, we'd say, "Ohmigod, I can't believe it! You're making $22,000 and you're only 22. Imagine when you're 40 and you're making $40,000!"

When I turned 40, I was so glad that didn't happen.

So, here I am, 22, making $22,000 a year and, yet, it didn't feel right. It didn't feel right. The first sign, as President Hennessy was saying, was when they tried to change my name. The news director said to me at the time, "Nobody's going to remember Oprah. So, we want to change your name. We've come up with a name we think that people will remember and people will like. It's a friendly name: Suzie."

Hi, Suzie. Very friendly. You can't be angry with Suzie. Remember Suzie. But my name wasn't Suzie. And, you know, I'd grown up not really loving my name, because when you're looking for your little name on the lunch boxes and the license plate tags, you're never going to find Oprah.

So, I grew up not loving the name, but once I was asked to change it, I thought, well, it is my name and do I look like a Suzie to you? So, I thought, no, it doesn't feel right. I'm not going to change my name. And if people remember it or not, that's OK.

And then they said they didn't like the way I looked. This was in 1976, when your boss could call you in and say, "I don't like the way you look." Now that would be called a lawsuit, but back then they could just say, "I don't like the way you look." Which, in case some of you in the back, if you can't tell, is nothing like Barbara Walters. So, they sent me to a salon where they gave me a perm, and after a few days all my hair fell out and I had to shave my head. And then they really didn't like the way I looked.

Because now I am black and bald and sitting on TV. Not a pretty picture.

But even worse than being bald, I really hated, hated, hated being sent to report on other people's tragedies as a part of my daily duty, knowing that I was just expected to observe, when everything in my instinct told me that I should be doing something, I should be lending a hand.

So, as President Hennessy said, I'd cover a fire and then I'd go back and I'd try to give the victims blankets. And I wouldn't be able to sleep at night because of all the things I was covering during the day.

And, meanwhile, I was trying to sit gracefully like Barbara and make myself talk like Barbara. And I thought, well, I could make a pretty goofy Barbara. And if I could figure out how to be myself, I could be a pretty good Oprah. I was trying to sound elegant like Barbara. And sometimes I didn't read my copy, because something inside me said, this should be spontaneous. So, I wanted to get the news as I was giving it to the people. So, sometimes, I wouldn't read my copy and it would be, like, six people on a pileup on I-40. Oh, my goodness.

And sometimes I wouldn't read the copy—because I wanted to be spontaneous—and I'd come across a list of words I didn't know and I'd mispronounce. And one day I was reading copy and I called Canada "ca nada." And I decided, this Barbara thing's not going too well. I should try being myself.

But at the same time, my dad was saying, "Oprah Gail, this is an opportunity of a lifetime. You better keep that job." And my boss was saying, "This is the nightly news. You're an anchor, not a social worker. Just do your job."

So, I was juggling these messages of expectation and obligation and feeling really miserable with myself. I'd go home at night and fill up my journals, 'cause I've kept a journal since I was 15—so I now have volumes of journals. So, I'd go home at night and fill up my journals about how miserable I was and frustrated. Then I'd eat my anxiety. That's where I learned that habit.

And after eight months, I lost that job. They said I was too emotional. I was too much. But since they didn't want to pay out the contract, they put me on a talk show in Baltimore. And the moment I sat down on that show, the moment I did, I felt like I'd come home. I realized that TV could be more than just a playground, but a platform for service, for helping other people lift their lives. And the moment I sat down, doing that talk show, it felt like breathing. It felt right. And that's where everything that followed for me began.

And I got that lesson. When you're doing the work you're meant to do, it feels right and every day is a bonus, regardless of what you're getting paid.

It's true. And how do you know when you're doing something right? How do you know that? It feels so. What I know now is that feelings are really your GPS system for life. When you're supposed to do something or not supposed to do something, your emotional guidance system lets you know. The trick is to learn to check your ego at the door and start checking your gut instead. Every right decision I've made—every right decision I've ever made—has come from my gut. And every wrong decision I've ever made was a result of me not listening to the greater voice of myself.

If it doesn't feel right, don't do it. That's the lesson. And that lesson alone will save you, my friends, a lot of grief. Even doubt means don't. This is what I've learned. There are many times when you don't know what to do. When you don't know what to do, get still, get very still, until you do know what to do.

And when you do get still and let your internal motivation be the driver, not only will your personal life improve, but you will gain a competitive edge in the working world as well. Because, as Daniel Pink writes in his best-seller, *A Whole New Mind*, we're entering a whole new age. And he calls it the Conceptual Age, where traits that set people apart today are going to come from our hearts—right brain—as well as our heads. It's no longer just the logical, linear, rules-based thinking that matters, he says. It's also empathy and joyfulness and purpose, inner traits that have transcendent worth.

These qualities bloom when we're doing what we love, when we're involving the wholeness of ourselves in our work, both our expertise and our emotion.

So, I say to you, forget about the fast lane. If you really want to fly, just harness your power to your passion. Honor your calling. Everybody has one. Trust your heart and success will come to you.

So, how do I define success? Let me tell you, money's pretty nice. I'm not going to stand up here and tell you that it's not about money, 'cause money is very nice. I like money. It's good for buying things.

But having a lot of money does not automatically make you a successful person. What you want is money and meaning. You want your work to be meaningful. Because meaning is what brings the real richness to your life. What you really want is to be surrounded by people you trust and treasure and by people who cherish you. That's when you're really rich.

So, lesson one, follow your feelings. If it feels right, move forward. If it doesn't feel right, don't do it.

Now I want to talk a little bit about failings, because nobody's journey is seamless or smooth. We all stumble. We all have setbacks. If things go wrong, you hit a dead end—as you will—it's just life's way of saying time to change course. So, ask every failure—this is what I do with every failure, every crisis, every difficult time—I say, what is this here to teach me? And as soon as you get the lesson, you get to move on. If you really get the lesson, you pass and you don't have to repeat the class. If you don't get the lesson, it shows up wearing another pair of pants—or skirt—to give you some remedial work.

And what I've found is that difficulties come when you don't pay attention to life's whisper, because life always whispers to you first. And if you ignore the whisper, sooner or later you'll get a scream. Whatever you resist persists. But, if you ask the right question—not why is this happening, but what is this here to teach me?—it puts you in the place and space to get the lesson you need.

My friend Eckhart Tolle, who's written this wonderful book called *A New Earth* that's all about letting the awareness of who you are stimulate everything that you do, he puts it like this: He says, don't react against a bad situation; merge with that situation instead. And the solution will arise from the challenge. Because surrendering yourself doesn't mean giving up; it means acting with responsibility.

Many of you know that, as President Hennessy said, I started this school in Africa. And I founded the school, where I'm trying to give South African girls a shot at a future like yours—Stanford. And I spent five years making sure that school would be as beautiful as the students. I wanted every girl to feel her worth reflected in her surroundings. So, I checked every blueprint, I picked every pillow. I was looking at the grout in between the bricks. I knew every thread count of the sheets. I chose every girl from the villages, from nine provinces. And yet, last fall, I was faced with a crisis I had never anticipated. I was told that one of the dorm matrons was suspected of sexual abuse.

That was, as you can imagine, devastating news. First, I cried—actually, I sobbed—for about half an hour. And then I said, let's get to it; that's all you get, a half an hour. You need to focus on the now, what you need to do now. So, I contacted a child trauma specialist. I put together a team of investigators. I made sure the girls had counseling and support. And Gayle and I got on a plane and flew to South Africa.

And the whole time I kept asking that question: What is this here to teach me? And, as difficult as that experience has been, I got a lot of lessons. I understand now the mistakes I made, because I had been paying attention to all of the wrong things. I'd built that school from the outside in, when what really mattered was the inside out.

So, it's a lesson that applies to all of our lives as a whole. What matters most is what's inside. What matters most is the sense of integrity, of quality and beauty. I got that lesson. And what I know is that the girls came away with something, too. They have emerged from this more resilient and knowing that their voices have power. And their resilience and spirit have given me more than I could ever give to them, which leads me to my final lesson—the one about finding happiness—which we could talk about all day, but I know you have other wacky things to do.

Not a small topic this is, finding happiness. But in some ways I think it's the simplest of all. Gwendolyn Brooks wrote a poem for her children. It's called "Speech to the Young : Speech to the Progress-Toward." And she says at the end, "Live not for battles won. / Live not for the-end-of-the-song. / Live in the along." She's saying, like Eckhart Tolle, that you have to live for the present. You have to be in the moment. Whatever has happened to you in your past has no power over this present moment, because life is now.

But I think she's also saying, be a part of something. Don't live for yourself alone. This is what I know for sure: In order to be truly happy, you must live along with and you have to stand for something larger than yourself. Because life is a reciprocal exchange. To move forward you have to give back. And to me, that is the greatest lesson of life. To be happy, you have to give something back.

I know you know that, because that's a lesson that's woven into the very fabric of this university. It's a lesson that Jane and Leland Stanford got and one they've bequeathed to you. Because all of you know the story of how this great school came to be, how the Stanfords lost their only child to typhoid at the age of 15. They had every right and they had every reason to turn their backs against the world at that time, but instead, they channeled their grief and their pain into an act of grace. Within a year of their son's death, they had made the founding grant for this great school, pledging to do for other people's children what they were not able to do for their own boy.

The lesson here is clear, and that is, if you're hurting, you need to help somebody ease their hurt. If you're in pain, help somebody else's pain. And when you're in a mess, you get yourself out of the mess helping somebody out of theirs. And in the process, you get to become a member of what I call the greatest fellowship of all, the sorority of compassion and the fraternity of service.

The Stanfords had suffered the worst thing any mom and dad can ever endure, yet they understood that helping others is the way we help ourselves. And this wisdom is increasingly supported by scientific and sociological research. It's no longer just woo-woo soft-skills talk. There's actually a helper's high, a spiritual surge you gain from serving others. So, if you want to feel good, you have to go out and do some good.

But when you do good, I hope you strive for more than just the good feeling that service provides, because I know this for sure, that doing good actually makes you better. So, whatever field you choose, if you operate from the paradigm of service, I know your life will have more value and you will be happy.

I was always happy doing my talk show, but that happiness reached a depth of fulfillment, of joy, that I really can't describe to you or measure when I stopped just being on TV and looking at TV as a job and decided to use television, to use it and not have it use me, to use it as a platform to serve my viewers. That alone changed the trajectory of my success.

So, I know this—that whether you're an actor, you offer your talent in the way that most inspires art. If you're an anatomist, you look at your gift as knowledge and service to healing. Whether you've been called, as so many of you here today getting doctorates and other degrees, to the professions of business, law, engineering, humanities, science, medicine, if you choose to offer your skills and talent in service, when you choose the paradigm of service, looking at life through that paradigm, it turns everything you do from a job into a gift. And I know you haven't spent all this time at Stanford just to go out and get a job. You've been enriched in countless ways. There's no better way to make your mark on the world and to share that abundance with others. My constant prayer for myself is to be used in service for the greater good.

So, let me end with one of my favorite quotes from Martin Luther King. Dr. King said, "Not everybody can be famous." And I don't know, but everybody today seems to want to be famous.

But fame is a trip. People follow you to the bathroom, listen to you pee. It's just—try to pee quietly. It doesn't matter, they come out and say, "Ohmigod, it's you. You peed."

That's the fame trip, so I don't know if you want that. So, Dr. King said, "Not everybody can be famous. But everybody can be great, because greatness is determined by service." Those of you who are history scholars may know the rest of that passage. He said, "You don't have to have a college degree to serve. You don't have to make your subject and verb agree to serve. You don't have to know about Plato or Aristotle to serve. You don't have to know Einstein's theory of relativity to serve. You don't have to know the second theory of thermodynamics in physics to serve. You only need a heart full of grace and a soul generated by love."

In a few moments, you'll all be officially Stanford's '08. You have the heart and the smarts to go with it. And it's up to you to decide, really, where will you now use those gifts? You've got the diploma, so go out and get the lessons, 'cause I know great things are sure to come.

You know, I've always believed that everything is better when you share it, so before I go, I wanted to share a graduation gift with you. Underneath your seats you'll find two of my favorite books. Eckhart Tolle's *A New Earth* is my current book club selection. Our *New Earth* webcast has been downloaded 30 million times with that book. And Daniel Pink's *A Whole New Mind: Why Right-Brainers Will Rule the Future* has reassured me I'm in the right direction.

I really wanted to give you cars but I just couldn't pull that off! Congratulations, '08!

Thank you.

OPRAH WINFREY

Wellesley Commencement Address
(1997)

My hat's off to you! My hat's off to you! You all have gone girls! I want to say thank you, Dr. Walsh and to the esteemed faculty, to those of you parents, what you have been through, God Bless you, and to the greatest class that has ever graduated from Wellesley.

I must say--you are my heart, Dr. Walsh is right. I saw you walking in and I started to weep, and I don't consider myself a weeper, but I guess I must be if I started to weep, because I know what it takes to get through here and I am so proud of all of you for getting through.

Thanks for inviting me to this party, this celebration. I told Dr. Walsh as we were walking in, my graduation was nothing like this. Nobody was having this much fun. When Wendy, Stedman's daughter, Stedman is my beau, my fiance, don't ask me when we're going to get married, when Stedman's daughter, Wendy, was looking for a school four years ago, no doubt I was far more delighted than she when she chose Wellesley 'cause I knew what she was in for.

I had wanted to come to this school. I wanted to be here but I could get no scholarship. I wanted to be here and have lived these past years vicariously through her. I was, as Dr. Walsh said, here with Wendy's father, Stedman, and Wendy's mother, Glinda, on Parents' Day and I was in awe of this place because, see, you all seem to have so much fun, without a keg or anything, and yet you all seemed so serious, so committed to this place with guts and with grace and I saw your sense of integrity and felt your intellect and realized that this was a very special, giving place.

Wellesley is a gift to any woman who is willing to open her mind and her heart to it. It is! You are so blessed to have had this, although I know your first year you maybe didn't think it was such a gift because I was there for a lot of those phone calls that Wendy made home. "Daddy (in small girl's voice), this is hard, they just want you to study all the time." Yes, they do. That was the Freshmen Year.

About mid-Sophomore Year, though, I think she had several epiphanies and realized what all of you had come to realize here that you do this for yourself, you don't do this for anybody else and that everything you heard about this institution is true--it is a prestigious and powerful place that will wear you out, but what happens is something--that Woman Thing starts to kick in around mid-Sophomore Year. We saw it kick in with Wendy, that Woman Thing that happens. She came here a naive girl from Dallas and Stedman and Glinda, I, and all of those who loved Wendy, are grateful to you Wellesley for the woman in process that you gave us back. We are grateful for that.

You could feel the change about a year and a half after her being here because she went from "Daddy (small girl's voice), this is hard," to "Daddy (adult voice), I won't be able to go on the trip to Africa because I have to study, Daddy." That Woman Thing!

You all know this, that life is a journey and I want to share with you just for a few moments about five things, aren't you glad they aren't ten, five things that have made this journey for me exciting, five lessons that I've learned that if I had gone to Wellesley I could have not made as many mistakes, but five lessons that I've learned that have helped me to make my life better.

First of all, life is a journey. I've learned to become more fully who you are and that is what I love about this institution, it allows women to come to the fullest extent of their possibilities of who they really are and that's what life does-- teach you to be who you are. It took me a while to get that lesson that it really is just about everyday experiences, teaching you, moment in, moment out, who you really are, that every experience is here to teach you more fully how to be who you really are.

Because, for a long time I wanted to be somebody else. I mean growing up I didn't have a lot of role models. I was born in 1954. On TV there was only Buckwheat, and I was ten years old before I saw Diana Ross on "The Ed Sullivan Show" with the Supremes and said I want to be like that and it took me a long time to realize I was never going to have Diana Ross's thighs, no matter how many diets I went on, and I was not going to have her hair neither unless I bought some and I came to the realization after being in television and having the news director trying to make me into something that I wasn't and going to New York and allowing myself to be treated less than I should have been--going to a beauty salon, you all know there is a difference between Black hair and White hair.

That is the one thing you learn the first week at Wellesley: how did you get your hair to do that? What I learned going to a beauty salon and asking them, after the news director told me that my hair was too thick and my eyes were too far apart and I needed a makeover, sitting in a French beauty salon, allowing them to put a French perm on my black hair and having the perm burn through my cerebral cortex and not being the woman that I am now, so not having the courage to say, this is burning me, and coming out a week later bald and having to go on the air. You learn a lot about yourself when you are Black, and a woman and bald and trying to be an anchor woman. You learn you are not Diana Ross and that you are not Barbara Walters who I was trying to be at the time.

I had a lot of lessons. I remember going on the air many times and not reading my copy ahead of time. I was on the air one night and ran across the word "Barbados," that may be Barbados to you but it was "Barb-a-does" to me that night and telling the story as an anchor woman about a vote in absentia in California, I thought it was located near San Francisco, and one of the worst, and this is when I broke out of my Barbara shell, because I am sitting there, crossing my legs, trying to talk like Barbara, be like Barbara, and I was reading a story about someone with a "blaze" attitude which, if I had gone to

Wellesley, I would have known it was blasé and I started to laugh at myself on the air and broke through my Barbara shell and had decided on that day that laughing was OK even though Barbara hadn't at that time. It was through my series of mistakes that I learned I could be a better Oprah than I could be a better Barbara and I allowed Barbara to be the mentor for me, as she always has been, and I decided then to try to pursue the idea of being myself and I am just thrilled that I get paid so much every day for just being myself, but it was a lesson long in coming, recognizing that I had the instinct that the inner voice that told me that you need to try to find a way to answer to your own truth was the voice I needed to be still and listen to.

One of the other great lessons I learned taught to me by my friend and mentor, Maya Angelou and if you can get this, you can save yourself a lot of time. Wendy and I have had many discussions about this, particularly when it comes to men, although she has a very nice one right now. Remember this because this will happen many times in your life.

When people show you who they are, believe them, the first time. Not the 29th time! That is particularly good when it comes to men situations because when he doesn't call back the first time, when you are mistreated the first time, when you see someone who shows you a lack of integrity or dishonesty the first time, know that that will be followed by many, many, many other times that will at some point in life come back to haunt or hurt you. Live your life from truth and you will survive everything, everything, I believe even death. You will survive everything if you can live your life from the point of view of truth.

That took me a while to get, pretending to be something I wasn't, wanting to be somebody I couldn't, but understanding deep inside myself when I was willing to listen, that my own truth and only my own truth could set me free. Turn your wounds into wisdom. You will be wounded many times in your life. You'll make mistakes. Some people will call them failures but I have learned that failure is really God's way of saying, "Excuse me, you're moving in the wrong direction." It's just an experience, just an experience.

I remember being taken off the air in Baltimore, being told that I was no longer being fit for television and that I could not anchor the news because I used to go out on the stories and my own truth was, even though I am not a weeper, I would cry for the people in the stories, which really wasn't very effective as a news reporter to be covering a fire and crying because the people lost their house (pretending to cry as she said this).

 And it wasn't until I was demoted as an on-air anchor woman and thrown into the talk show arena to get rid of me, that I allowed my own truth to come through. The first day I was on the air doing my first talk show back in 1978, it felt like breathing, which is what your true passion should feel like. It should be so natural to you. And so, I took what had been a mistake, what had been perceived as a failure with my career as an anchor woman in the news business and turned it into a talk show career that's done OK for me!

Be grateful. I have kept a journal since I was 15 years old and if you look back on my journal when I was 15,16, it's all filled with boy trouble, men trouble, my daddy wouldn't let me go to Shoney's with Anthony Otie, things like that. As I've grown older, I have learned to appreciate living in the moment and I ask that you do, too.

I am asking this graduating class, those of you here, I've asked all of my viewers in America and across the world to do this one thing. Keep a grateful journal. Every night list five things that happened this day, in days to come that you are grateful for. What it will begin to do is to change your perspective of your day and your life. I believe that if you can learn to focus on what you have, you will always see that the universe is abundant and you will have more. If you concentrate and focus in your life on what you don't have, you will never have enough. Be grateful. Keep a journal. You all are all over my journal tonight.

Create the highest, grandest vision possible for your life because you become what you believe. When I was a little girl, Mississippi, growing up on the farm, only buckwheat as a role model, watching my grandmother boil clothes in a big, iron pot through the screen door, because we didn't have a washing machine and made everything we had. I watched her and realized somehow inside myself, in the spirit of myself, that although this was segregated Mississippi and I was "colored" and female, that my life could be bigger, greater than what I saw.

I remember being four or five years old, I certainly couldn't articulate it, but it was a feeling and a feeling that I allowed myself to follow. I allowed myself to follow it because if you were to ask me what is the secret to my success, it is because I understand that there is a power greater than myself, that rules my life and in life if you can be still long enough in all of your endeavors, the good times, the hard times, to connect yourself to the source, I call it God, you can call it whatever you want to, the force, nature, Allah, the power. If you can connect yourself to the source and allow the energy that is your personality, your life force to be connected to the greater force, anything is possible for you. I am proof of that. I think that my life, the fact that I was born where I was born, and the time that I was and have been able to do what I have done speaks to the possibility. Not that I am special, but that it could be done.

Hold the highest, grandest vision for yourself. Just recently we followed Tina Turner around the country because I wanted to be Tina, so I had me a nice little wig made and I followed Tina Turner because that is what I can do and one of the reasons I wanted to do that is Tina Turner is one of those women who have overcome great obstacles, was battered in her life, and like a phoenix rose out of that to have great legs and a great sense of herself. I wanted to honor other women who had overcome obstacles and to say that Tina's life, although she is this great stage performer, Tina's life is a mirror of your life because it proves that you can overcome.

Every life speaks to the power of what can be done. So I wanted to honor women all over the country and celebrate their dreams and Tina's tour was called the Wildest Dreams Tour. I asked women to write me their wildest dreams and tell me what their wildest dreams were. Our intention was to fulfill their wildest dreams. We got 77,000 letters, 77,000. To our disappointment we found that the deeper the wound the smaller the dreams.

So many women had such small visions, such small dreams for their lives that we had a difficult time coming up with dreams to fulfill. So we did fulfill some. We paid off all the college debt, hmmm, for a young woman whose mother had died and she put her sisters and brothers through school. We paid off all the bills for a woman who had been battered and managed to put herself through college and her daughter through college.

We sent a woman to Egypt who was dying of cancer and her lifetime dream was to sit on a camel and use a cell phone. We bought a house for another woman whose dream had always been to have her own home but because she was battered and had to flee with her children one night, had to leave the home seventeen years ago. And then we brought the other women who said we just wanted to see you, Oprah, and meet Tina, that was their dream! Imagine when we paid off the debt, gave the house, gave the trip to Egypt, the attitudes we got from the women who said I just want to see you. And some of them afterwards were crying to me saying that we didn't know, we didn't know, and this is unfair, and I said, that is the lesson: you needed to dream a bigger dream for yourself. That is the lesson. Hold the highest vision possible for your life and it can come true.

I want to leave you with a poem that I say to myself sometimes when I am feeling a little down, although I really don't get down a lot because I know that every experience when it happens, something difficult comes into my life, I say what is it you're here to teach me and what I try to do in my life is to get God on the whisper. He always whispers first.

Try to get the whisper before the earthquake comes because the whisper is always followed by a little louder voice, then you get a brick I say, and then sometimes a brick wall, and then the earthquake comes. Try to get it on the whisper. But Maya Angelou wrote a poem and I don't know a poem more fitting than Phenomenal Woman for this crowd because you are and these words are for you.

She says, "Pretty women, honey, they wonder just where my secret lies `cause I'm not cuter, built to suit a fashion model size but when I start to tell them, they say, Girl, you're telling lies and I said, no, honey, it's in the reach of my arms, it's in the span of my hips, it's in the stride of my stepping, it's in the curl of my lips, `cause I'm a woman, honey, phenomenally, phenomenal, phenomenal woman.

OPRAH WINFREY

Sometimes I walk into a room just as cool as you please and to a man the fellows either stand up or fall down on their knees. And then they start swarming all around me like a hive of honey bees and I said whoopcha must be this fire in my eyes, could be the flash of my teeth or the swing of my waist or just the joy in my feet, all I know is I'm a woman, you're a woman, we are women, honey, phenomenally, phenomenal women.

Now you understand why my head's not bowed, you won't see me dropping about or when you see me coming, it ought to make you proud, sister girl, I say, it's the bend of my hair, it's in the palm of my hands, the need for your care 'cause I'm a woman, you're a woman, we just women, we are phenomenal, phenomenally phenomenal, phenomenal women.

That's you, Wellesley, that's you.

God Bless You!

OPRAH WINFREY

Harvard Commencement Speech

(2013)

Oh my goodness! I'm at Harvard! Wow! To President Faust, my fellow honorans, Carl [Muller] that was so beautiful, thank you so much, and James Rothenberg, Stephanie Wilson, Harvard faculty, with a special bow to my friend Dr. Henry Lewis Gates. All of you alumni, with a special bow to the Class of '88, your hundred fifteen million dollars. And to you, members of the Harvard class of 2013! Hello!

I thank you for allowing me to be a part of the conclusion of this chapter of your lives and the commencement of your next chapter. To say that I'm honored doesn't even begin to quantify the depth of gratitude that really accompanies an honorary doctorate from Harvard. Not too many little girls from rural Mississippi have made it all the way here to Cambridge. And I can tell you that I consider today as I sat on the stage this morning getting teary for you all and then teary for myself, I consider today a defining milestone in a very long and a blessed journey. My one hope today is that I can be a source of some inspiration. I'm going to address my remarks to anybody who has ever felt inferior or felt disadvantaged, felt screwed by life, this is a speech for the Quad.

Actually I was so honored I wanted to do something really special for you. I wanted to be able to have you look under your seats and there would be free master and doctor degrees but I see you got that covered already. I will be honest with you. I felt a lot of pressure over the past few weeks to come up with something that I could share with you that you hadn't heard before because after all you all went to Harvard, I did not. But then I realized that you don't have to necessarily go to Harvard to have a driven obsessive Type A personality. But it helps. And while I may not have graduated from here I admit that my personality is about as Harvard as they come. You know my television career began unexpectedly.

As you heard this morning I was in the Miss Fire Prevention contest. That was when I was 16 years old in Nashville, Tennessee, and you had the requirement of having to have red hair in order to win up until the year that I entered. So they were doing the question and answer period because I knew I wasn't going to win under the swimsuit competition. So during the question and answer period the question came "Why, young lady, what would you like to be when you grow up?" And by the time they got to me all the good answers were gone. So I had seen Barbara Walters on the "Today Show" that morning so I answered, "I would like to be a journalist. I would like to tell other people's stories in a way that makes a difference in their lives and the world." And as those words were coming out of my mouth I went whoa! This is pretty good! I would like to be a journalist. I want to make a difference. Well I was on television by the time I was 19 years old. And in 1986 I launched my own television show with a relentless determination to succeed at first. I was nervous about the competition and then I became my own competition raising the bar every year, pushing, pushing, pushing myself as hard as I knew. Sound familiar to anybody here? Eventually we did make it to the top and we stayed there for 25 years.

The "Oprah Winfrey Show" was number one in our time slot for 21 years and I have to tell you I became pretty comfortable with that level of success. But a few years ago I decided, as you will at some point, that it was time to recalculate, find new territory, break new ground. So I ended the show and launched OWN, the Oprah Winfrey Network. The initials just worked out for me. So one year later after launching OWN, nearly every media outlet had proclaimed that my new venture was a flop. Not just a flop, but a big bold flop they call it.

I can still remember the day I opened up USA Today and read the headline "Oprah, not quite standing on her OWN." I mean really, *USA Today*? Now that's the nice newspaper! It really was this time last year the worst period in my professional life. I was stressed and I was frustrated and quite frankly I was actually I was embarrassed. It was right around that time that President Faust called and asked me to speak here and I thought you want me to speak to Harvard graduates? What could I possibly say to Harvard graduates, some of the most successful graduates in the world in the very moment when I had stopped succeeding? So I got off the phone with President Faust and I went to the shower. It was either that or a bag of Oreos. So I chose the shower. I was in the shower a long time and as I was in the shower the words of an old hymn came to me. You may not know it. It's "By and by, when the morning comes." I started thinking about when the morning might come because at the time I thought I was stuck in a hole. And the words came to me "Trouble don't last always" from that hymn, "this too shall pass." And I thought as I got out of the shower I am going to turn this thing around and I will be better for it. And when I do, I'm going to go to Harvard and I'm going to speak the truth of it! So I'm here today to tell you I have turned that network around!

And it was all because I wanted to do it by the time I got to speak to you all so thank you so much. You don't know what motivation you were for me, thank you. I'm even prouder to share a fundamental truth that you might not have learned even as graduates of Harvard unless you studied the ancient Greek hero with Professor Nagy. Professor Nagy as we were coming in this morning said, "Please Ms. Winfrey, walk decisively."

I shall walk decisively.

This is what I want to share. It doesn't matter how far you might rise. At some point you are bound to stumble because if you're constantly doing what we do, raising the bar. If you're constantly pushing yourself higher, higher the law of averages not to mention the Myth of Icarus predicts that you will at some point fall. And when you do I want you to know this, remember this: there is no such thing as failure. Failure is just life trying to move us in another direction.

Now when you're down there in the hole, it looks like failure. So this past year I had to spoon feed those words to myself. And when you're down in the hole, when that moment comes, it's really okay to feel bad for a little while. Give yourself time to mourn what you think you may have lost but then here's the key, learn from every mistake because every experience, encounter, and particularly your mistakes are there to teach you and force you into being more who you are. And then figure out what is the next right move. And the key to life is to develop an internal moral, emotional G.P.S. that can tell you which way to go.

Because now and forever more when you Google yourself your search results will read "Harvard, 2013". And in a very competitive world that really is a calling card because I can tell you as one who employs a lot of people when I see "Harvard" I sit up a little straighter and say, "Where is he or she? Bring them in." It's an impressive calling card that can lead to even more impressive bullets in the years ahead: lawyer, senator, C.E.O., scientist, physicist, winners of Nobel and Pulitzer Prizes or late night talk show host. But the challenge of life I have found is to build a résumé that doesn't simply tell a story about what you want to be but it's a story about who you want to be. It's a résumé that doesn't just tell a story about what you want to accomplish but why.

A story that's not just a collection of titles and positions but a story that's really about your purpose. Because when you inevitably stumble and find yourself stuck in a hole that is the story that will get you out. What is your true calling? What is your dharma? What is your purpose? For me that discovery came in 1994 when I interviewed a little girl who had decided to collect pocket change in order to help other people in need. She raised a thousand dollars all by herself and I thought, well if that little 9-year-old girl with a bucket and big heart could do that, I wonder what I could do? So I asked for our viewers to take up their own change collection and in one month, just from pennies and nickels and dimes, we raised more than three million dollars that we used to send one student from every state in the United States to college. That was the beginning of the Angel Network.

And so what I did was I simply asked our viewers, "Do what you can wherever you are, from wherever you sit in life. Give me your time or your talent your money if you have it." And they did. Extend yourself in kindness to other human beings wherever you can. Together we built 55 schools in 12 different countries and restored nearly 300 homes that were devastated by hurricanes Rita and Katrina. So the Angel Network — I have been on the air for a long time — but it was the Angel Network that actually focused my internal G.P.S. It helped me to decide that I wasn't going to just be on TV every day but that the goal of my shows, my interviews, my business, my philanthropy all of it, whatever ventures I might pursue would be to make clear that what unites us is ultimately far more redeeming and compelling than anything that separates me.

Because what had become clear to me, and I want you to know, it isn't always clear in the beginning because as I said I had been on television since I was 19 years old. But around '94 I got really clear. So don't expect the clarity to come all at once, to know your purpose right away, but what became clear to me was that I was here on Earth to use television and not be used by it; to use television to illuminate the transcendent power of our better angels. So this Angel Network, it didn't just change the lives of those who were helped, but the lives of those who also did the helping. It reminded us that no matter who we are or what we look like or what we may believe, it is both possible and more importantly it becomes powerful to come together in common purpose and common effort.

I saw something on the "Bill Moore Show" recently that so reminded me of this point. It was an interview with David and Francine Wheeler. They lost their 7-year-old son, Ben, in the Sandy Hook tragedy. And even though gun safety legislation to strengthen background checks had just been voted down in

Congress at the time that they were doing this interview they talked about how they refused to be discouraged. Francine said this, she said, "Our hearts are broken but our spirits are not. I'm going to tell them what it's like to find a conversation about change that is love, and I'm going to do that without fighting them." And then her husband David added this, "You simply cannot demonize or vilify someone who doesn't agree with you, because the minute you do that, your discussion is over. And we cannot do that any longer. The problem is too enormous.

There has to be some way that this darkness can be banished with light." In our political system and in the media we often see the reflection of a country that is polarized, that is paralyzed and is self-interested. And yet, I know you know the truth. We all know that we are better than the cynicism and the pessimism that is regurgitated throughout Washington and the 24-hour cable news cycle. Not my channel, by the way. We understand that the vast majority of people in this country believe in stronger background checks because they realize that we can uphold the Second Amendment and also reduce the violence that is robbing us of our children. They don't have to be incompatible.

And we understand that most Americans believe in a clear path to citizenship for the 12,000,000 undocumented immigrants who reside in this country because it's possible to both enforce our laws and at the same time embrace the words on the Statue of Liberty that have welcomed generations of huddled masses to our shores. We can do both.

And we understand. I know you do because you went to Harvard. There are people from both parties, and no party, [who] believe that indigent mothers and families should have access to healthy food and a roof over their heads and a strong public education because here in the richest nation on Earth, we can afford a basic level of security and opportunity. So the question is, what are we going to do about it? Really, what are you going to do about it? Maybe you agree with these beliefs. Maybe you don't. Maybe you care about these issues and maybe there are other challenges that you, Class of 2013, are passionate about. Maybe you want to make a difference by serving in government. Maybe you want to launch your own television show. Or maybe you simply want to collect some change. Your parents would appreciate that about now. The point is your generation is charged with this task of breaking through what the body politic has thus far made impervious to change. Each of you has been blessed with this enormous opportunity of attending this prestigious school. You now have a chance to better your life, the lives of your neighbors and also the life of our country. When you do that let me tell you what I know for sure. That's when your story gets really good.

Maya Angelou always says, "When you learn, teach. When you get, give. That my friends is what gives your story purpose and meaning." So you all have the power in your own way to develop your own Angel Network and in doing so, your class will be armed with more tools of influence and empowerment than any other generation in history. I did it in an analog world. I was blessed with a platform that at its height reached nearly 20,000,000 viewers a day.

Now here in a world of Twitter and Facebook and YouTube and Tumblr, you can reach billions in just seconds. You're the generation that rejected predictions about your detachment and your disengagement by showing up to vote in record numbers in 2008. And when the pundits said, they said they talked about you, they said you'd be too disappointed, you'd be too dejected to repeat that same kind of turnout in 2012 election and you proved them wrong by showing up in even greater numbers. That's who you are.

This generation, your generation I know, has developed a finely honed radar for B.S. Can you say "B.S." at Harvard? The spin and phoniness and artificial nastiness that saturates so much of our national debate. I know you all understand better than most that real progress requires authentic — an authentic way of being, honesty, and above all empathy. I have to say that the single most important lesson I learned in 25 years talking every single day to people, was that there is a common denominator in our human experience.

Most of us, I tell you we don't want to be divided. What we want, the common denominator that I found in every single interview, is we want to be validated. We want to be understood. I have done over 35,000 interviews in my career and as soon as that camera shuts off everyone always turns to me and inevitably in their own way asks this question "Was that okay?" I heard it from President Bush, I heard it from President Obama. I've heard it from heroes and from housewives. I've heard it from victims and perpetrators of crimes. I even heard it from Beyonce and all of her Beyonceness. She finishes performing, hands me the microphone and says, "Was that okay?"

Friends and family, yours, enemies, strangers in every argument in every encounter, every exchange I will tell you, they all want to know one thing: was that okay? Did you hear me? Do you see me? Did what I say mean anything to you? And even though this is a college where Facebook was born my hope is that you would try to go out and have more face-to-face conversations with people you may disagree with.

That you'll have the courage to look them in the eye and hear their point of view and help make sure that the speed and distance and anonymity of our world doesn't cause us to lose our ability to stand in somebody else's shoes and recognize all that we share as a people. This is imperative, for you as an individual, and for our success as a nation. "There has to be some way that this darkness can be banished with light," says the man whose little boy was massacred on just an ordinary Friday in December.

So whether you call it soul or spirit or higher self, intelligence, there is I know this, there is a light inside each of you, all of us, that illuminates your very human beingness if you let it. And as a young girl from rural Mississippi I learned long ago that being myself was much easier than pretending to be Barbara Walters. Although when I first started because I had Barbara in my head I would try to sit like Barbara, talk like Barbara, move like Barbara and then one night I was on the news reading the news and I called Canada "Can-a-da," and that was the end of me being Barbara. I cracked myself up on TV. Couldn't start laughing and my real personality came through and I figured out, oh gee, I can be a much better Oprah than I could be a pretend Barbara.

I know that you all might have a little anxiety now and hesitation about leaving the comfort of college and putting those Harvard credentials to the test. But no matter what challenges or setbacks or disappointments you may encounter along the way, you will find true success and happiness if you have only one goal, there really is only one, and that is this: to fulfill the highest most truthful expression of yourself as a human being. You want to max out your humanity by using your energy to lift yourself up, your family and the people around you. Theologian Howard Thurman said it best. He said, "Don't ask yourself what the world needs.

Ask yourself what makes you come alive and then go do that, because what the world needs is people who have come alive." The world needs … People like Michael Stolzenberg from Fort Lauderdale. When Michael was just 8 years old Michael nearly died from a bacterial infection that cost him both of his hands and both of his feet. And in an instant, this vibrant little boy became a quadruple amputee and his life was changed forever.

But in losing who he once was Michael discovered who he wanted to be. He refused to sit in that wheelchair all day and feel sorry for himself so with prosthetics he learned to walk and run and play again. He joined his middle school lacrosse team and last month when he learned that so many victims of the Boston Marathon bombing would become new amputees, Michael decided to banish that darkness with light. Michael and his brother, Harris, created Mikeysrun.com to raise $1 million for other amputees — by the time Harris runs the 2014 Boston Marathon. More than 1,000 miles away from here these two young brothers are bringing people together to support this Boston community the way their community came together to support Michael. And when this 13-year-old man was asked about his fellow amputees he said this, "First they will be sad. They're losing something they will never get back and that's scary. I was scared. But they'll be okay. They just don't know that yet."

OPRAH WINFREY

We might not always know it. We might not always see it, or hear it on the news or even feel it in our daily lives, but I have faith that no matter what, Class of 2013, you will be okay and you will make sure our country is okay.

I have faith because of that 9-year-old girl who went out and collected the change. I have faith because of David and Francine Wheeler, I have faith because of Michael and Harris Stolzenberg, and I have faith because of you, the network of angels sitting here today. One of them Khadijah Williams, who came to Harvard four years ago. Khadijah had attended 12 schools in 12 years, living out of garbage bags amongst pimps and prostitutes and drug dealers; homeless, going in to department stores, Wal-Mart in the morning to bathe herself so that she wouldn't smell in front of her classmates, and today she graduates as a member of the Harvard Class of 2013.

From time to time you may stumble, fall, you will for sure, count on this, no doubt, you will have questions and you will have doubts about your path. But I know this, if you're willing to listen to, be guided by, that still small voice that is the G.P.S. within yourself, to find out what makes you come alive, you will be more than okay. You will be happy, you will be successful, and you will make a difference in the world. Congratulations Class of 2013. Congratulations to your family and friends. Good luck, and thank you for listening. Was that okay?

On Career, Life and Leadership
at Stanford Graduate School of Business
(2014)

Oprah: Love, love, love. Tweet, tweet. Thank you! So happy to be in the bubble. Love it! Aren't you all the luckiest people in the world? Oh my god! I envy you. Hi, Amanda.

Amanda: Hi Oprah. So we have been so excited and eagerly anticipating this day. This campus has been buzzing since the announcement was made last week that you'd be coming here.

Oprah: Thanks for the buzz. I'm so glad I still have a buzz. So good.

Amanda: I received a lot of support and advice from my friends and that was really great. I just wanted to say, I think the best advice I heard was don't worry Amanda if you mess up Oprah can just interview herself. So if I falter, feel free to ask yourself some questions and we'll begin. But to get things started, I thought we'd frame today's talk with framing three sections with quotes of yours that you shared, after wrapping up your 25th season and final season of the Oprah Winfrey Show. I thought some of these quotes, I mean you share so much wisdom, but these really spoke to me and that would be a great way to frame our discussion.

So this first one that I will read for everyone and for you, so you don't have to strain your neck, is that 'You have to know what sparks the light in you, so that you in your own way can illuminate the world.' So I wanted to take this time to talk about your early career and how you discovered your calling. So let's go back to when you were college age. Did you know that you wanted to get into TV and media specifically?

Oprah: No, I did not. I thought that I was going to be a teacher. I was in my sophomore class at Tennessee State University. I'd already been working in radio since I was 16 and I remember I was in Mr. Cox's Drawing class for theater. I was terrible drawer, he said I couldn't draw a straight line with a ruler. I got a call in that class from a guy at the local station, CBS, and he'd been calling me several times. When I was working in radio, I started working in radio at 16. I won the Miss Fire Prevention Contest, another long story. So when I went back to the station to pick up my prize, some guy said would you like to hear your voice on tape? I said sure and I started reading this copy on tape.

They called everybody in the building, said hear this kid read. I was 16, they hired me in radio. I was in radio at 16 and so I started getting calls about my freshman year to come into television. I had never thought about it. Still was living at home and couldn't figure out how I would manage those- I had biology at one o'clock. I couldn't figure out how I would be able to manage my schedule. Mr. Cox said to me, the same professor who said you can't draw a straight line with a ruler. I came back from taking this phone call and he said, who was that? I said there's this guy at CBS, he keeps calling me, he wants me to interview for a job. Mr. Cox said, that is why you go to school fool, so that CBS can call you! That is why you're in school!

He said, you leave now and go call him back. I did and I was hired in television, not knowing anything about it. Having in mind Barbara Walters, but thinking oh okay, I can do that. Not knowing how to write or film or anything. I think it was because it was the times and I literally had somebody who was willing to work with me, that I managed to find my way. But I had to find my way because the reporting never really fit me. What did work for me, I'm this old. I'm so old that when I started that it was a year of live action camera.

So it was like video cameras live and so the news stations would do a live shot. They would throw to somebody live, even if nothing was going on. Just so they could say, live action cam! What I found is I wasn't so good at the writing part, but if I was just standing up and talking about what had just happened, it was really good. So I started at 19 working in television, became an anchor immediately afterwards. My father still had an 11 o'clock curfew, can you believe such a thing? That I am the 10 o'clock anchor in Nashville, Tennessee. I am the woman on the newscast reading the news and my father would say be home by 11. I'd say, 'Dad the news is on at 10.' He goes, 'and it's off at 10 30, so be home by 11.' I had a very strict father, anyway I could feel inside myself that reporting was not the right thing for me, even though I was happy to have the job.

I got an offer to go to Atlanta. I was making $10,000 a year in 1971, but still in college. I was thinking I was doing pretty good. I got an offer to go to Atlanta for 40,000, which I thought it's over! I'm going to make $40,000! My boss at the time said to me, 'you do not know what you don't know. You need to stay here until you can learn to write better until you can perfect your craft as a journalist. He said, 'We can't give you 40, but we can give you 12.' I stayed and the reason why I stayed is because I could feel inside myself that even though the 40 was alluring at the time that he was absolutely right. To make a long story short, cause I'd be here all day just talking about how it all came about. I started listening to what felt like the truth for me.

A couple of years later, I moved to Baltimore. I could feel that as a reporter and by this time 22, I'm making 22,000. I met my best friend Gayle there who said, 'oh my God! Can you imagine if you're 30 and you're making 30,000? Then you're 40 and then it's 40,000! We actually had that conversation in the bathroom. I started to feel that reporting wasn't for me. But I had my father, I had my friends, everybody was saying, oh my God! You're an anchor woman, you're on TV. I mean you can't give up that job.

By the time I was making 25, my father goes, 'well you just hit the jackpot. You're not going to make no more money than that.' I was torn between what the world was saying to me and what I felt to be the truth for myself. It felt like an unnatural act for me reporting, although I knew that a lot of people, it was glamorous. I started to just inside myself, think, what do I really want to do? What I really want to do? I will say this, knowing what you don't want to do is the best possible place to be if you don't know what to do. Because knowing what you don't want to do, leaves you to figure out what is it you really do want to do.

Amanda: So you discovered talk then, right? Around that time.

Oprah: I didn't discover talk, I got demoted. They wanted to fire me, but I was under contract. They didn't want to give up the 25,000. They were trying to keep me on to the end of the year. This is the way life works.

They put me on a talk show to try to avoid having to pay me the contract out. The moment I sat on the talk show interviewing the Carvel ice cream man and his multiple flavors, I knew that I had found home for myself. Because when I was a news reporter, it was so unnatural for me to cover somebody's tragedies and difficulties and then to not to feel anything for it. I would go back after a fire and I would take them blankets and then I would get a note from my boss saying, what the hell are you doing?

Oprah: You're just supposed to report it.

Amanda: You can't be that empathetic.

Oprah: You cannot be that empathetic and it felt unnatural for me. If I were to put it in business terms or to leave you with a message that the truth is I have from the very beginning, listened to my instinct. All of my best decisions in life have come because I was attuned to what really felt like the next right move for me. It didn't feel right, I knew that I wouldn't be there forever. I never even learned the streets in Baltimore because I thought I was there longer than I thought. I was there eight years, I should've learned the streets. But I kept saying to myself. I'm not going to be here long. I'm not going to be here, so I'm not going to learn the streets. When I got the call to come to Chicago, after starting with a co-anchor and working in talk for several years, I knew that it was the right thing to do. I knew that even if I didn't succeed, because at the time there was a guy named Phil Donahue who was the King of Talk and was on Chicago and every single person, except my best friend, Gayle, said you're going to fail. Every single person. My bosses, by this time thought I was terrific and said, you're walking into a landmine, you're going to fail. You're going to fail. Chicago is a racist city. You're black, you're not going to make it. Everything to keep me staying they even offered me a car and an apartment and all this stuff. I said, no, if I fail, then I will find out what is the next thing for me. What is the next true thing for me.

Amanda: It felt right to you, so you went for it.

Oprah: Because it felt like this is now the move I need to make. I was not one of those people, you know the people who worked with me in news, they would have their tapes and they'd have their stories and they'd have resumes ready. I didn't have any of that because I knew that the time would come where what I needed would show up for. When that showed up, I was ready. Because my definition of luck is preparation meeting the moment of opportunity. I was prepared to be able to step into that world of talk, in a way that I knew I could do it.

Amanda: Right. Often in your career, I'm sure you are a minority. Perhaps as the only woman, the only black person, the only person from a poor family. Did this affect you on your professional path? How did you navigate situations in which you might've felt more alone? Now, how did that impact how you lead and how you might help people who may be feeling that same thing?

Oprah: Okay, man, that's a lot of questions.

Amanda: I'm sorry.

Oprah: I mean I have to put my glasses on.

Amanda: I figured I had you here. I was going to ask as much as I could.

Oprah: Amanda went deep on me there for a minute there, whoa! Backup sister, girl, come on back up. First one is?

Amanda: How did you navigate situations in which you might've felt more alone?

Oprah: Always the only woman in the room. Still walk in the only woman in the room and there's a room full of white men, usually older. Thrills me, just thrills me. I just love it! Usually the only black person in the room. Also never really concerned me because I don't look at people through color. I didn't get to be where I am and who I am by looking at the color of people's skin. I really literally took Martin Luther King at his word, and understand that the content of a person's character and refuse to let anybody else do that to me. So I love it! Just love it! There's a wonderful phrase by Maya Angelou, from a poem that she wrote called, To our Grandmothers. That she says, 'When I come as one, but I stand as 10,000.'

So when I walk into a room and particularly before I have something really challenging to do. Or I'm going to be in a circumstance where I feel I'm going to be up against some difficulties. I will literally sit, and I will call on that 10,000. I will call on the ancestors, I will call on those people who've come before me. I will call on the women who forged a path that I might be able to sit in the room with all of those white men and love it so much. I call on that because I know that my being where I am, first of all, being who I am and where I am, didn't come just out of myself. That I come from a heritage and so I own that. I step into that room, not just as myself, but I bring all of that energy with me.

It has never been an issue for me, except when I was I think 23, still working in Baltimore. I'd gone to my boss and said that the guy who was working with me, my cohost on the People are Talking Show, was making more money than I. We were co-hosts. I went to my boss, and I said, this is in 1970, so I was older than 23. It was 1979, 80 and I said, I just would like to, you know how intimidating it is to go to the boss in, the first place. But I'm going to go and I'm going to stand up for myself. I said, Richard's making more money than I am, and I don't think that's fair because we're doing the same job, we sit in the same show.

My general manager said, 'why should you make as much money as he?' I said, cause we're doing the same job. He said, 'but he has children, do you have children?' I said no, he said, 'well he has to pay for college education. So he owns his own home, do you own your home?' I said no. He said, 'He has a mortgage to pay, he has insurance, do you have that?' No. 'So tell me why do you need the same amount of money? And I said, 'thank you for your time,' and I left, I left. I didn't complain about it. I didn't file a suit about it. I knew that in that moment, it was time for me to go. That I started the process for myself, of preparing myself, for you will not be here long. You are not going to be able to get what you need.

I had a boss at the time who was African American and had just been for the first time, made an assistant news director and was drunk with power. Drunk with power and felt it his. I don't know, I think he woke up in the morning, thinking of things he could do to harass me. I decided not to file a suit against it because I knew at the time I would lose. That no good would come of it. That I would be blackballed in television, that it would turn into a major thing. I knew I didn't have long to stay there. I had a vision for what the future was, even though I couldn't place exactly where my future would be. I knew who held the future, because I am really guided by a force that's bigger than myself. I know that my being here on the planet is not just in my own making.

Amanda: So you use that as momentum to just leave. Cut your losses and go?

Oprah: No I just said, I filed it away. I go, there will come a time.

Amanda: Yes you were right. I think you were right.

Oprah: When I will be sitting in the same room and it happened like in the late nineties, I had the Oprah Show, and I ran into that guy. Lord Jesus. Thank you! Oh, one of the sweetest moments I've ever had. Go ahead.

Amanda: Here we go. Right now as we sit here, we're about five miles from Facebook and Sheryl Sandberg. Last year she published the book 'Lean In', and it has gotten incredible traction. It had some criticism as well, and I was wondering if you were to write a book on women and careers, what would your title be?

Oprah: Mine would be actually, mine wouldn't be Lean In, it would be, "Step Up and Into Yourself." Because this is the truth, there is no real doing in the world without being first. For me, being your presence, your connection to yourself, and that which is greater than yourself, is far more important than what you do. But also is the thing that fuels what you do. I know that one of the things that is so important for what happens here at the graduate school is that you have leaders who are self-actualized and understand what your contribution to change the world can be. You can only do that if you know yourself. You cannot do it unless you take the time to actually know who you are and why you are here. Now, I happen to know for sure that every human being comes called and that the calling goes beyond their definition of what your job is. There is an innate, supreme moment of destiny for everybody. That's why when I was in Baltimore, I could feel this isn't it, this isn't it.

Then in Chicago, after 25 years of success on the show, I started to feel this isn't it, there's something more. Something more that's calling me to what is the Supreme moment. Everybody has that and you cannot fulfill it unless you have a level of self-awareness. To be connected to what is the inner voice or the instinct, I call it your emotional GPS system that allows you to make the best decisions for yourself. Every decision that has profited me has come from me listening to that inner voice first, and every time I've gotten into a situation where I was in trouble, it's because I didn't listen to it.

I overrode that voice, that instinct with my own head, my own thinking. I tried to rationalize it. I tried to tell myself, you're going to make a lot of money. Oh no! I sit here profitable, successful by all the definitions of the world. But what really resonates deeply with me is that I live a fantastic life. My inner life is really intact, I live from the inside out. Everything that I have, I have because I let it be fueled by who I am and what I realized my contributions to the planet could be. What my real contribution is, it looks like I was a talk show host. It looks like I'm in the movies. It looks like I have a network, but my real contribution, the reason why I'm here is to help connect people to themselves and the higher ideas of consciousness.

I'm here to help raise consciousness, so my television platform was to help raise consciousness. In the beginning. I didn't realize that. I thought, oh my God! I got a show! It wasn't until I was interviewing the Ku Klux Klan one day, and can you imagine all the great lessons come from things that are sometimes challenging. I was interviewing the Ku Klux Klan and I thought as an African American, oh, I'm going to get them! I'm going to show for every Jewish person, for every person who's been discriminated against. During the commercial break, I saw the clan exchanging signals and looks at each other. Then something inside, that instinct, I thought I am doing nobody any good. They are loving this, they are using me. I think I'm doing an interview, they are using me. I did not know it at the time, I brought them on actually, those same guys back in for my last year. They told me that they use that show for their recruitment, I could feel that happening.

I made a decision after that show, I'll never do anything like that again. I'll never let my platform be used and I will not be used. At the time in the nineties, early nineties, everybody was doing confrontational television. I thought I was above the fray cause I'm not like Jerry Springer, I don't do that. So in my egoic delusion, I thought because I am not that bad, I'm really not bad. But I was doing confrontational television. I thought

I was exposing men with affairs: we happened to have a guy on who was talking about how he'd had an affair with his wife. He was crazy enough to come on with his wife and his girlfriend. People ask me, why do people do that? It's because nobody ever asked him. So you said, would you come on with your wife and your girlfriend? He goes, sure!

Amanda: He was thinking.

Oprah: He was thinking. So he comes on with the wife and the girlfriend. This is a life-changing moment for me, the clan and this woman. The wife is there, he's in the center and the girlfriend, and he tells, he announces, we were live television at the time. He announced to the world and to his wife, that his girlfriend was pregnant. And I, you see your face? Your mouth's open right there. I did exactly that, I went, oh my God! You could hear the gasp in the audience, I literally, really it still makes my eyes water when I think about it. I looked at her face and I felt her humiliation. I felt her shame, I felt it. I said never again. I will get out of television if I have to do this. I went and I had a meeting with the producers because I just had the Klan before, and I got the adulterers here. Some uplifting show, I must say.

I said to the producers, we are going to change, we're going to turn this around. I'm no longer going to be used by television, I am going to use television. What a concept! I'm going to use television as a force, I didn't say at the time for good. I said, let's think about what we want to say to the world and how we want to use this as a platform to speak to the world. How do we want to see the world change? How do we want to impact the world and then let all of our shows really be focused and centered around that. I then said to the producers exactly what I said to you backstage, do not bring me a show unless you have fully thought out, what is your intention for doing it. Because if there is a religion or a mantra or law that I live by, I live by the third law of motion in physics. Which is for every action there's an equal and opposite reaction.

That is my religion. I know that what I'm thinking and therefore going to act on, is going to come back to me in a circular motion, just like gravity. What goes up, comes down. What also propels the action is the intention, so I don't do anything without being fully clear about why I intend to do it. Because the intention is going to determine the reaction, the result or the consequence in every circumstance, I don't care what it is. I said to my producers, come to me with your intention at whatever it is, whatever shows you're proposing, whatever ideas you're proposing and then I will decide based upon the intention, do I really want to do that. Is this how we want to use this platform? That really is the secret to why we were number one all those years is because it was intention fueled, intention based coming out of purposeful programming. Yes, that's what it was.

Amanda: Great. That's a perfect segue to go to our second section, which I read this quote and it just struck me as so true and I wanted to delve into it. "I've talked to nearly 30,000 people on this show and all 30,000 had one thing in common, they all wanted validation. I will tell you that every single person you will ever meet shares that common desire." Oprah, you are a true Renaissance woman. You have your own network, you had this amazingly successful show for 25 years. You've been in movies, you are one of the most important philanthropists of our time.

Oprah: Oh I love hanging around you! I'm just taking it all in really.

Amanda: I love it too so!

Oprah: The part I love the most is a Renaissance woman. As you said that I went, what does that really mean? I don't know, but I like it!

Amanda: I was a history major, so it seemed like a natural.

Oprah: I'm a Renaissance woman, who knew! Okay.

Amanda: Go ahead. Good! I'm glad you like it. What are the qualities of your leadership that make you successful at such diverse pursuits? What works for in one area that maybe doesn't work in another?

Oprah: Well, I tell you it works in all areas because my life is fueled by my being. The being fuels the doing. So I come from a centered place, I come from a focused place. I come from compassion, it's just my nature. I come from a willingness to understand and to be understood. I come from wanting to connect. I mean the secret of that show for 25 years, is that people could see themselves in me. All over the world, they could see themselves in me. Even as I became more and more financially successful, which was a big surprise to me. It was like, oh my God! This is so exciting.

Amanda: You mean you got more than that 30,000?

Oprah: I got more than 30,000, by the time it was 30. But what I realized is through the whole process, because I'm grounded in my own self. That although I could have more shoes, my feet stayed on the ground, although I was wearing better shoes. I can keep my feet on the ground, even though I could get more shoes and I could understand that it really was because I was grounded. I've done, was doing and continue to this day to do the consciousness work. I work at staying awake and being awakened is just another word for spirituality, but spirituality throws people off and they think, you mean religion.

When I was hiring people for my company for OWN, looking for presidents. When people would come in I'd say, tell me, what is your spiritual practice? Literally with throat, people would go well, I'm not religious. I said I didn't ask you about your religion. I asked you what your spiritual practice? What do you do to take care of yourself? What do you do to keep yourself centered? What do you do? One woman started crying, you know that's not the person.

Amanda: So that's a sign.

Oprah: That's a sign. So to answer your question, everything is fueled that comes from me, really wanting to be a better person on earth. This is what I know to be true. The reason why the show worked is because I understood that, that audience, my viewers, the people who watched us every day and would come and just like you all did. Get tickets and they would come, you all just came across campus, but that's good too. But people would come from all over the world just to be there with their aunts and their mothers. They'd come with their cousins and there'd be a few men in there going, what the hell am I doing? Or saying well, I went to Oprah with you, I went to Oprah. At least get me clear for three or four weeks. I went to Oprah with you.

I had such regard for that, and I just had a conversation with John Mackey who runs Whole Foods. He has written this fabulous book, you should get it called Conscious Capitalism. He was talking about how the investment in the stakeholders, the people who you are serving, that connection between the people who you're trying to serve and sell to is equally as important as the people who you're buying from.

Equally as important as the people who are supporting you financially as your stockholders if you are a public company. I always understood that there really was no difference between me and the audience. At times I might've had better shoes, but at the core of what really matters, that we are the same. You know how I know that? Because all of us are seeking the same thing. You're here at this fabulous school and will go out into the world and each pursue based upon what you believe your talents are. What your skills are, maybe your gifts are, but you're seeking the same thing. Everybody wants to fulfill the highest truest expression of yourself as a human being, that's what you're looking for. The highest truest expression of yourself as a human being.

Because I understand that if you're working in a bakery and that's where you want to be and that may be what you've always wanted to do is to bake pies for people. Or bake cakes for people, or to offer your gift, then that's for you. There's no difference between you and me, except that's your platform, that's your show every day. My understanding of that has allowed me to.

Amanda: Reach everyone.

Oprah: To reach everyone. There's no way that you wouldn't because that's what I truly feel. When I sit down to talk to somebody, whether I'm talking to a murderer. I sat down, I interviewed a guy who'd killed his twin daughters. I've interviewed child molesters, trying to figure out what it is they do and why they do it. Obviously, lots of people who've been victimized through molestation. Presidents, politicians, Beyonce herself, at the end of every interview, the murderer to Beyonce, the question everybody asks that you mentioned is what that okay? How was that? Everybody says that and I now just wait for it. Is that okay? Was that okay? When I finish, I'll say to you, was that okay?

Amanda: I'm going to ask you too.

Oprah: Okay. You're very okay. You're doing very well.

Amanda: Oh thank you.

Oprah: Very okay. Very, okay. What I started to feel, feel sense is that there's a common thread that runs through every interview. It doesn't matter what it is or what it is about, everybody wants to know, and this is the truth. All of your arguments are really about the same thing: it's about did you hear me? Did you see me? And did what I say mean anything to you? That's what everything is about. The reason why I left my boss's office when I was asking for a raise, I knew he didn't hear nor see me neither, and that I was not going to get the validation that I needed. Now, I couldn't articulate that at the time. I just knew let me get out of here. But now I know, I could feel inside myself, I'm not going to get the validation that I'm looking for.

I also know that's what every human being is looking for. They're looking to know, are you fully here with me? Are you fully here or are you distracted? That's what your children want to know, that's what the people you work for want to know. That's what you want to know, is did you hear me? Every argument isn't about whatever it is you think you're arguing about, it's really about, but can you hear me? And many people have even said it, have you not said it? You're not hearing me.

You're not hearing me. So having that understanding, and I would have to say that the show. One of the reasons why I live such a fantastic life is because I pay attention. I pay attention to my life and your life is your greatest teacher. Every single thing that's happening to you every day, your joys, your sadness, your challenges, your worries. Everything is happening to bring you closer to in here. Everything is trying to take you home to yourself and when you're at home with yourself, when you're solidly there, connected to whatever you call creation. Even if you don't call it anything, connected to an energy force, that has unlimited power for you. When you can connect it to that, you are your best.

One of my greatest lessons came from a guy who wrote a book called Seat to the Soul. I was doing them on the show, and I started talking this consciousness, spiritual talk, two months after I started the show. My producers would all be like, oh God! There she goes again! But I knew that even though masses of people were not tuning in for that, that the whole purpose of that platform was to try to lift people up. Now I have a network and I can articulate what it is I'm trying to do. I'm trying to bring little pieces of light into people's lives, because what is my job? My job is not to be an interviewer, my job is not to be a talk show host, or just to own a network. I am here to raise the level of consciousness, to connect people to ideas and stories so that they can see themselves and live better lives.

Amanda: Thank you. I want to shift gears. And focus a bit on philanthropy.

Oprah: Are you worried about getting all your stuff in?

Amanda: No, we're doing great. We're just going to keep going. I think everyone likes this right? We're good. I watched your interview with the Forbes Conference on Philanthropy, and you said something really interesting, which was that early on, some of your biggest mistakes in giving were, because you made emotional decisions.

Yet we learn here at the GSB, like one of the crucial messages we take away with us, is that it's really important to be, as you said before self-aware. To be understanding often to share our emotions with others and you yourself have been the master of harnessing vulnerability with yourself and your guests over the years. How do you strike a balance between emotion and logic? How do you make sure that you're making logical decisions when you're giving.

Oprah: Oh, these are so well thought out, these questions.

Amanda: Thank you.

Oprah: Okay. Let me think about that for a moment. Very good. Okay. Well, I would have to say that you need both: you need emotion, and you need logic. In the beginning I was purely emotional, made a lot of mistakes. I happened to be sitting, I was sharing this story with Dean Solemner, just before he came on. I was sitting in Nelson, Mandela's living room and I'm not just saying that's a name drop, I was actually sitting there.

Amanda: You stayed with him, right?

Oprah: I stayed with him for 10 days and as I said to the Dean and Lisa, I literally could have written a book called 29 meals. Cause I had 29 meals with him at that particular time.

I didn't record it. So something I think was at the second meal or the 12th meal anyway. I was sitting with Madiba, and we were talking about how do you really make an impact in the world. We were reading the paper and I'd reached a point where I was no longer like, oh my God! What am I going to say? We were just sitting in silence reading the paper and there was an article in the paper about some tragic situation. We both started talking about the way to end poverty is through education. I said to him, I really at some point would like to build a school over here and then he got up and called the Minister of Education and said, get over here now! Oprah wants to build a school. I was like, well I was thinking about it, I didn't say I wanted to do it today, but we literally started the process then.

It was an emotional decision for me in that I think philanthropy should come out of you. Your doing should come out of your being. Everybody knows my story as a poor Negro child growing up in apartheid Mississippi and if it were not for education and being born at the right time. Because I was literally born in the year of desegregation, five years before three years before, two years before, nobody would have even had the hope that my life could have been any different. Because I was born at that time and literally moved out of Mississippi by the time I was in my first classroom. I was in kindergarten, wrote my kindergarten teacher a letter, Ms. New. I said, Dear Miss New, I do not belong here because I know a lot of big words and then I wrote every big word I knew. Elephant, hippopotamus, Mississippi, Nicodemus, Shadrach, Meshach, and Abednego from the Bible. Ms. New said, who did this? I said I did, so then they marched me off to the principal's office. Only time I was ever in there, principal's office. Principal made me sit and write those words again and I got myself out of kindergarten into first grade. First grade skipped, second grade. Heller! The Renaissance began.

Amanda: You've always had this conviction. It seems like you've always known who you are, even if you weren't finding it.

Oprah: I knew I didn't belong there.

Amanda: You knew that.

Oprah: With those kids. In kindergarten, you're sitting there, that's what I'm telling you to listen to your instinct. You look around and you see these kids, they are playing with some blocks.

Amanda: They all do that.

Oprah: And I know Nicodemus, I do not think I belong in here. I do not belong in here, my point is education really opened the door as we all know, not going to give you the education speech. How do you change a person's life? I had prior to starting my school in South Africa, I had this big idea that I was going to emotional. That I was going to take all a hundred families out of the projects and green and green, and I was going to give them a new life and I was going to buy them homes. That did not work. It failed miserably. I had a big sister program that I started, failed miserably. I realized that for me, first of all, I realized you don't change as you all are recognizing through the seed program.

You first have to change the way a person thinks and sees themselves. You've got to create a sense of aspiration, a sense of hopefulness so a person can see. Can begin to even have a vision for a better life and if you can't connect to that, then you lose. You lose and they lose and it's just money after money. For me, it's using my philanthropy to do what I have found to be enormously helpful. You know, the light in my life was education. So for me, in the beginning when I started to make money, especially when it's published, everybody and their brother calls you.

Then you've got to make a decision, am I going to do what everybody else wants me to do? Or am I going to be led by who I really am? I learned as will happen to anybody who's successful in your family, people start treating you like the First National Bank. You've got to decide, you've got to draw the boundaries for yourself and decide how are you going to use your money, your talent, your time in such a way that it's going to serve you first. Because if it doesn't allow you to be filled up, then you get depleted and you no longer want.

Amanda: Right and you can't keep doing it.

Oprah: You can't keep doing it. My decisions are now emotional and logical, meaning I choose education, but I do it in such a way that's actually going to benefit the person that I'm serving. Then it's not just, oh, I want to help people, you know?

Amanda: Thank you. To move on to our last part, you said at the end of your 25 years, 'Gratitude is the single greatest treasure I will take with me from this experience.' Now you've started your own network and you continue to be very involved in your philanthropy and your school, is there anything left that you're scared to try?

Oprah: Whoa, Amanda! You must've been up all night long.

Amanda: I prepared a little bit.

Oprah: Oh my goodness. Anything left that I'm scared to try? No. I'm just trying to think, well is there something that I hadn't thought of?

Amanda: Cause there's not much you haven't done.

Oprah: But I stay in my lane. I know what my lane is. I know that my real calling is what I said earlier. I know what it looks like to the rest of the world. Oh talk shows does that, but I really know what I'm here to do, which is the number one thing I would say to you. First, let me answer your question, so no, there's nothing I'm not scared to try. I have hit my stride, but I haven't done what I ultimately came to do. There still is a Supreme moment of destiny that awaits me.

I also knew that during the Oprah show, I've kept a journal since I was 15 years old. It's so pitiful when you go back and see how pathetic you were as a person sometimes. But I always knew, even during that show, that the show, we live in a fame culture, we live in a fame-centered world, had this literally been during the Renaissance people would have valued different things. If we'd been doing the transcendentalist period, people valued different things.

But in our culture, we value fame. I always understood that that was the basis for me being known in the world because people wouldn't be able to hear you unless you came with some swag or swagger you know. I also understood that that was just the foundation to be heard, but that there was a lot more to be said. For me, owning a network or being a part of a network is about continuing to use that platform to raise the consciousness. I do a show on Sundays, which you can stream live called Super Soul Sunday, where I literally talked to thought leaders from around the world and ask the questions, not as good as you, I'm going to consult with you.

Ask the questions in life that really matter, to get people thinking about what really matters in their lives. The responses that I get from people just regarding that show, let me know that I'm on the right track, I'm moving in the right direction. I'm not afraid, because I know that all of us have a limited time here, but the real question is who are you and what do you want to do with it? How are you going to use who you are.

My favorite line from Seat of the Soul, is when the personality comes to serve the energy of your soul, that is authentic empowerment. As graduates of this great school, to take what you've learned here, to take what is a part of your nature and what you've developed as skills and what really feeds your passion. To take that and to align that with the deeper potential and possibility of your soul's coming.

When you align your personality with what your soul came to, and everybody has it, align your personality with your purpose, and nobody can touch you. You wake up every day and you are fired up. It's like, oh my God, another day! It's so great! Because everybody has a purpose, so your whole thing is to figure out what that is. Your real job is to figure out why you're really here and then get about the business of doing that.

Amanda: Oprah, thank you so much.

Oprah: Are we going to take some questions?

Amanda: Yes, so that's what I wanted to say. I'd love to put it out.

Andre: Hernandez, asks Oprah, who has been your favorite interviewee and why?

Oprah: Well, actually I would have to say there's so many over the years. The truth is that the people whose names that I can't even remember, and you probably wouldn't remember, have been the most revelatory, the most impactful. I mean watching people step out of tragedies and defined triumph for themselves, those people really have been the ones that really shaped me and made me a better human being. I did an interview once with a woman and actually with Dr. Phil, where she had come to the show and was planning to kill herself afterwards. She said because her daughter had been murdered eight years before and she couldn't get past it. She just wanted to come on the Oprah show and talk about it.

And Phil said to her, why do you spend all your time lamenting, all these years of lamenting the death instead of celebrating the life. You've let the one day define your daughter's entire life and she looked up at him and she said, you know I never thought about it that way before with tears. I could feel the shift in her. So the most important moments for me have been, when literally I can see that somebody has made a shift in the way they see themselves in the world. Or you know what we call now an aha moment, those I live for that. I live for that, those are my favorite interviews.

Audience Member: Hi Oprah. My name is Melissa and I wanted to know how do you think about balancing selflessness with selfishness.

Oprah: Why are you asking me that question?

Audience Member: It's kind of the tension between putting yourself first. And also taking care of others.

Oprah: Okay. Well, I would say this, everybody's heard the whole oxygen mask thing. The truth is you don't have anything to give that you don't have. You have to keep your own self-full ,that's your job. You know one of my daughters is here today from Oprah Winfrey Leadership Academy. Stand up Chaday so everybody can see you. You're going to end your first year soon. Oh my God! The first year! I say to my girls, all of the time, that your real work is to figure out where your power base is and to work on the alignment of your personality, your gifts that you have to give with the real reason why you're here. That's the number one thing you have to do is to work on yourself and to fill yourself up and keep your cup full, keep yourself full. Now, I used to be afraid of that. I used to be afraid, particularly from people who say, oh, she's so full of herself. She's so full and now I embrace it. I consider it a compliment that I am full of myself.

Because only when you're full, I'm full I'm overflowing my cup runneth over. I have so much, I have so much to offer and so much to give, and I am not afraid of honoring myself. You know it's miraculous when you think about it. First of all, for me, my father and mother never married. They had sex one time underneath an oak tree because she was wearing a poodle skirt in 1953. My dad to this day, says I want to know what's under that skirt, that's what I want to know. He wanted to know what was under the skirt, they didn't really have a relationship. She wanted one, but you know he went under the skirt and then that was it. One time under the oak tree, bam! Renaissance woman is born. It happened there.

Oprah: That's why I know my life is bigger than that. My life has to be bigger as yours is, bigger than a moment, than the poodle skirt. It's much bigger, the design, the reason why I'm here is much bigger than, oh, I think I want to see what's under that. The ability to take care of that, to honor that, to honor yourself and that which is greater than yourself, that which was the reason for your being here. There's no selflessness in that, because only through that, do you have the ability to offer yourself, your whole self, your full expression of who you are to the rest of the world. I remember the very first time I had a life coach, they weren't called that at the time. But the expert on who shared with our audience, the women, she did a list and say, where are you on the list? Literally in that audience, women booed her, when she said, put yourself top of the list.

This was in 1992, in 1992 the idea of being top of your own list was people like, how dare she? She doesn't have children. I said, she didn't say abandon your children and go running in the streets. She just said, put yourself at the top of the list, nurture yourself, honor yourself. Stop the crazy mind chatter in your head that tells you all the time that you're not good enough, because that's the number one I found too, issue with everybody.

The reason people say, you know, how was that? How was that? Is because you want to know, how do you measure up? Well, to know that you're just being here. You're just being here. However that sperm, bam! Hit that egg. However, that occurred for you, that your being here is such a miraculous thing and that your real job is to honor that, is to honor that.

The sooner you figure that out. Oh wow! Wow! I'm one of the lucky ones, I got to be here. How do you continue to prepare yourself to live out the highest, fullest, truest expression of yourself as a human being. I just want to end with this. There are no mistakes. There really aren't any, because you have a Supreme destiny. When you're in your little mind, in your little personality mind where you're not centered. Where you really don't know who you are, that you come from something greater and bigger, and that we really all are the same. When you don't know that you get all flustered, you get stressed all the time, wanting something to be what it isn't. There's a Supreme moment of destiny calling on your life, your job is to feel that, to hear that, to know that. Sometimes when you're not listening, you get taken off track. You get in the wrong marriage, the wrong relationship, you take the wrong job. Yes, but it's all leading to the same path. There are no wrong paths, there are none.

There's no such thing as failure really, cause failure is just that thing trying to move you in another direction. You get as much from your losses as you do from your victories, because the losses are there to wake you up. The losses would say fool, that is why you go to school. So that CBS can call you! So when you understand that you don't allow yourself to be completely thrown by a grade or by a circumstance, because your life is bigger than any one experience.

I always ask people on Super Soul Sunday, tell me what would you say to your younger self? Every person says in one form or another, I would have said relax. Relax, it's going to be okay. It really is going to be okay because even if you're on a detour right now, and that's how you know, when you're not at ease with yourself. When you're feeling like, oh, that is the cue that you need to be moving in another direction. Don't let yourself get all thrown off, continue to be thrown off course, when you're feeling off course, that's the key. How do I turn around?

When everybody was talking about, when I started this network, if I had only known good Lord, how difficult it would be. The way through the challenge is to get still and ask yourself, what is the next right move? Not think about, oh, I got all of this stuff.

What is the next right move? Then from that space, make the next right move and the next right move and not to be overwhelmed by it. Because you know, your life is bigger than that one moment. You know you're not defined by what somebody says is a failure for you, because failure is just there to point you in a different direction.

Amanda: Thank you.

Speech at Power of Women
(2015)

Thanks Aves. That was so good. You know all those years, 25 years of doing the Oprah Show and going into work at 5:30 in the morning in the makeup chair by 6:30. Literally crawling home at night for 25 years, I used to wonder what the ladies who lunch were doing. Really, I was attracted to paintings of women lunching and so this is what it's like, but even better, this is an empowerment lunch. I changed how I viewed power about 1989. There was a book I read by a man named Gary Zuckav called Seat of the Soul and in Seat of the Soul, he defined what is true power, what is authentic power. His definition of authentic power, meaning the kind of power that can never be taken from you. Not your looks, not your fame, not your money, not your square footage, but authentic power is when the personality, your personality comes to serve the energy of your soul. When you are able to align who you are, who you've become in the world, with really what you've come to do in the world, when your personality serves the soul.

I thought a lot about that, that book was actually life-changing for me. I was building a home in Santa Barbara and as anybody who's ever built a bathroom or a home or anything, nothing ever happens on time. It was 2002 and we're supposed to be finished and it wasn't finished, and I was like, I can't wait to get in the house. I'm finally going to have a great Christmas and I'm going to do the kind of Christmas that I dreamed of.

From the Currier and Ives cards, I'm going to have the wreaths on the door. But I didn't have a floor, so it was a little difficult to do that. I started to think if I can't do that Christmas, well, what am I going to do for Christmas? My house isn't even ready and what can I do? I started as I was walking around through the trees sitting under that tree. Cause my favorite time is to be alone with my thoughts. As I was alone with my thoughts, I was thinking what would be the next best possible Christmas for myself? I thought of the best Christmas I ever had, the best Christmas I ever had was when I was 12 years old.

My mother was on welfare. I was living with my mother and half-brother and sister in Milwaukee. My mother called me into a room to say, we won't be having Christmas this year. I said, we won't be having Christmas, what about Santa Claus? There is no Santa Claus. I had already figured that out, but okay. I was embarrassed and I was ashamed, because for the first time I had to face the reality that yes, what I've been suspecting that we're not like the other kids, that we are really poor is true. So we're not going to have Christmas and there is no Santa Claus. My first thought after being embarrassed and ashamed was what will my story be? What am I going to tell everybody when we go back to school and they're showing their toys and I don't have anything to talk about. What am I going to do? I'm not going to go outside tomorrow. When everybody's out in the yards, showing the toys they got for Christmas, I'm going to stay inside. Am I going to pretend I'm sick? What is my story going to be?

Well, late that night, some nuns showed up at our house and they brought the basket of food and they brought toys for my brother and my sister. I was overwhelmed with joy that those nuns showed up, not because they brought me a Tammy doll, when I really wanted a Barbie doll. I was overwhelmed because somebody remembered that we existed, and somebody cared enough in the middle of the night to come to our house with food and toys and also I would now have a story. As I was contemplating, that was the best Christmas I ever had, I thought, how could I make that possible for somebody else? What could I do to create the same kind of experience for other children? I took 50 members of my team at Harpo, Harriet one of them, Sherri, and hired another 50 people in South Africa. We went to South Africa with the idea of creating something that we ended up doing a documentary about, called Christmas Kindness. Christmas Kindness, using my personality to serve the energy of my soul.

We went from village to village, offering toys and clothes, food, soccer balls to children who'd never experienced Christmas before. Early in the morning, you could see them lining up by the thousands to come and we actually went to 10 or 12 villages to do this. People said to me at the time, oh, that's so frivolous and the kids won't remember it and why don't you use your money to do something else more substantial Oprah? I said they may not remember the toy. They may not remember the clothes, although they were most excited, the children to open boxes, containing clothes. Because as their caretaker said to us, having new clothes made them not feel poor and for so many of these kids was the first time they'd ever experienced having something new for them. They may not remember what they got in the box, but they will remember that somebody remembered them. They will remember the experience.

During this entire experience, Nelson Mandela had invited Stedman and I to stay at his home. So when Nelson Mandela invites you, you stay, and I was so nervous. I was like, oh my God! What am I going to talk about because it's 10 days. It's 10 days, it's not just a dinner. It's not a lunch, it's 10 days. It's 10 days, breakfast, lunch, and dinner with Nelson Mandela. What am I going to say? Stedman said, why don't you try listening? So I did, I had 29 meals with Nelson Mandela. At first, really, I was very like, oh my God, It's Nelson Mandela. By the third or fourth day, he and I were to sit together in his living room, sharing the paper at the end of the day, talking about events in the world. One of the things we came to talk about the most was the power of education to overcome poverty. In one of those lucid moments, I said to him, well you know, I've always wanted to build a school. He said, "you want to build a school? Oprah, you want to build a school." He got up and made a phone call to the Minister of Education. I wasn't planning on building it then, but all right.

The Minister of Education comes over later in the day and we start the process of building a school. The reason why I wanted to build a school because I tried different things. Because I always knew even before I could articulate it, that my personality needs to serve my soul. I always knew that to whom much is given, as the Bible says, much as expected. Not just expected, much is required. From the first time I came to Chicago and started to make more money than I needed to actually pay my bills. I reached out and was going to form a sister group trying to help young girls in the project. I discovered I wasn't able to do what I really needed to change the trajectory of those girls' lives. Because every girl that we would take out of the project and spend time with on the weekends, my producers and I, they would have to go back home into the same environment. It was impossible to just change the way they saw themselves in the world.

By trial and error, I knew that in order to literally change the way a girl sees herself, I would need enough time to spend with her. To be able to hire the right kind of teachers, the right kind of administration, to be surrounded by a nurturing environment to allow that girl to change the way she felt about herself and saw herself in the world. The idea of creating a boarding school that was surrounded by beauty, the kind of school that I would want to go to. I tell you, when I first sat down with the architects and said, I want to build a great school. A great school for leaders that will change the lives of women, and they will be able to break the cycle of poverty for themselves and their families forever and become a part of the real and true, new and free South Africa. Well, the architect said to me, well, these are poor girls. These girls, I said well, where are the closets? Where's the space? Where's the drama? Where's the theater? They said, well, these poor girls, these girls really don't come from families with clothes and a lot of them have lost their families. I said, but they will have clothes and they will be able to do drama and they will be able to excel beyond anybody's dreams.

That is exactly what has happened five years later. As Ava mentioned we are now approaching, I'll go over at the end of November, for our fifth graduating class. This coming June, I'll have 43 girls graduating in South Africa. I have seven in the United States graduating. I have 20 girls in the United States. One of them Shadae is here today. Stand up Shadae, say hi, this young woman, who's now a junior at Stanford, I met when she was 12 years old, I did the interview and said, tell me why you want to come. Do you want to come to this school? She says, I really want to come. I really, really want to come. A dozen reallys and she has done magnificent work throughout seventh grade, eighth grade, 10th grade, 12th grade. From the moment my goddaughter Kirby, who's also here today, who's Gail's daughter, came to speak to the girls at the school. Kirby was attending Stanford and from the moment Shadae heard Kirby speak about Stanford, she said that she knew that those were her people.

We went to Stanford and looked at the campus, she said, Mamo, these are my peeps. This is what I know, that being here today and hearing from Susan and Gwyneth and Selma and Rebecca and Jim and Anna and all of us, it's a really good thing. But I have always known this about celebrity. The real power of being somebody that somebody knows, and I really think that the only difference between being famous and not, is that more people know your name. The only difference between understanding, that is understanding that what Selma has done, what Susan has done, what Anna has done, Rebecca has done, what Jim has done, what I've done, you too can do. Because true philanthropy comes from living from the heart of yourself and giving what you have been given. How will you do that? How will you use your personality, the energy of your personality to serve that, which is your soul's calling.

I know this for sure, any life, no matter how fantastic it is, how glorious it seems, how much attention you receive, how much square footage you have. Any life and every life is enhanced by the sharing and the giving and the opening up of the heart space. Your life gets better when you can find a way to share it with someone else. What we've done, you can do. The real empowerment comes when every person leaves this room and makes a decision. Maybe that decision is that you will write a check and support some of the wonderful organizations you've heard here today. But the true decision is how will you use yourself? How will you use everything that you have been given to serve that which is greater than yourself? How will you use that to become truly, authentically empowered? Now it is a beautiful thing to receive an award and to be on the cover of Variety. Thank you very much. It's a beautiful thing, but the true reward is in the lives that you are able to touch and the people who, you have impacted.

My beloved mentor, teacher, friend, mother, Maya Angelou passed away last year. I remember when I opened the school, I was so happy that finally it happened, we got it done and got through all the bureaucracy and all the stuff that it takes to build a school from the ground up. I said to Maya, oh my God, Maya! This is my legacy. Maya said, "you have no idea. You have no idea what your legacy is." Your legacy is every life you have touched. Your legacy is every person you have met, whose influence was felt by you. Every single person she said, it's every person who's ever watched a show and decided that they were going to go back to school or watched a show and decided that I'm going to leave my husband. I'm going to not no longer be a victim of abuse. Every person who watched a show and said, I am a victim of abuse and because I saw this, I now can stand up for myself. Every person who gained a voice because of you, you have no idea what your legacy is. Your legacy is every life that you touched.

As you leave here today, the decision is whose lives will that be? How will you use yourself in such a way, that your impact and your legacy will live beyond the doing. The great reward for me is knowing that what I'm doing and how I've done it and how I choose to live in the space that I call God. How in God I move and breathe and have my being and I try to move from the center, that is able to literally touch the lives of other people. I said to the girls, when they first came to the school, we found them in villages, we found them in townships. We went out, some kids were having school in a box car on a railroad track and some under a tree. I said to the girls, the trajectory of your life is about to change, and I only ask one thing of you, is that you give as much of yourself as I, and the school is willing to give to you. Becky Sykes who is head of our foundation and spent so much, stand up Becky. Spent so much time with the girls, they can vouch for this.

So this is the true reward, I just wanted to share this with you. One of my Shadae is here, because she's the only one of the 20 girls who are in school in the United States. Girls range from Brown, Mount Holyoake. Wellesley, Johnson, C. Smith, Spellman, Colorado, Oregon, Stanford. She's the only one that had Fridays off, so I said everybody, not getting out of class to come to Variety. But June of this year, the girls are out in the world. We've done this thing that Susan was talking about, touching the lives of girls. When you change a girl's life, you don't just change a girl's life, you change the community's life. You change a family's life because what girls do is they take it back home. They take it to their families, they take it to their communities. My girls are all over the country in internships and working and doing multiple things during the summer months. One of my daughters, I call them my daughters, Avokile, who's at Colorado College was working, went back to Cape Town, to work in Cape Town this summer. She'd always want it to be a doctor and planned to major in medicine in the summer, made the decision that she was going to switch to public health. When they leave, I always say just let me know, just send a text. You don't even have to say you arrived just send an emoji, emoji, hello, I'm here. But she wrote me this amazing letter that will be something I treasure forever. I just wanted to share a bit of it with you today. She wrote this on June 11th after having arrived in Cape Town and being in a house with all of these students from different parts of the world.

She writes, "This is a girl whom we found who would have had a very different life." But she writes, "The other day, we were all sitting around the table and began to have a heated, passionate, respectful and compassionate and most important, fulfilling discussion about what we want our own country and our nation to be." "What we should be doing as the youth of this country to make it better." For the first time, I really believe I have hope for a better future. We talked about what male privilege means, what white privilege means and the chains of victimization." "Oh, my Mamo, it was challenging yet so insightful. It felt good to know that I could share my opinion with a group of only guys and know that if my opinion was disagreed upon, it was solely because of the quality of my opinion and not because I'm a girl." "I'm finding myself being able to let go and be me without fear of what the next person thinks. When I think I can go deep with someone, I do and most of the time it turns out that person was also seeking the same thing. I'm learning, I'm making mistakes. I'm laughing, I'm deciding, I'm asking and I'm questioning and I'm also growing. I have to tell you, I am filled with gratitude, so much gratitude that I can see the sights, that I can see and meet the people I have met and continued to be favored by God." That's the true reward. Thank you.

OPRAH WINFREY

Keynote Speech at QuickBooks Connect
(2015)

Oprah: Hello! I am so happy to be here with all you thinking business people. First of all, shout out to Leah who took an Essence cover. There you are Leah, thank you so much. To Katie, who I just met backstage a little while ago. Katie raising three kids, grew up poor, I grew up poor. I said Katie, isn't growing up poor fantastic? It's fantastic because it makes you dream bigger. I just want to say thank you to the team at Intuit, because when you first called me and asked me to speak about creating a brand, building a brand, what my brand means to me. I saw this tweet today, discover the best way to build a brand from the woman who wrote the book on it, see Oprah's keynote.

I actually had an LOL moment when I saw that. For real, because there's nobody who has resisted being a brand more than I. Why? I will tell you why. I resisted being a brand, because I thought that when people started to tell me that I was a brand and I get interviewed in the early nineties and people say, well you are a brand, tell us about your brand. I'd say no, I'm not a brand, I'm a person. I felt that being a brand somehow was going to corporatize me and I would no longer have the connection to the audience and people would think of me as like this corporation and not really as the person that I saw myself connecting to the audience. Then I ran into a woman at Kroger, we're in the frozen food section. I was wearing flip-flops and she said, you that lady on TV? I said yes and she goes, oh, I don't think you come out looking like that. I said, this is my day off.

She said, I want to tell you a story, I used to hear you all the time talk about not beating your kids. The first time I heard you say nobody should beat their kids, I said she don't have no kids. Cause how you going to have kids if you don't beat them. She goes, that's the first time I heard you say it. And then I saw another show you did, and you was again, you was on there talking about don't beat your kids. I go, there she goes again talking about don't beat your kids, she don't have no kids. It wasn't the first time or the second time, but every time I saw you do a show about raising kids, you always said we shouldn't beat that kid. So I said, one day I'm going to try, I'm going to try for one week not to hit my kid. I went one week I didn't hit my kid, then I went another week. I say I going to try another week. I'm going to not hit my kid, no matter what he does.

Now it's been six months and I haven't hit my kid. I have a different kid and I'm a different person. Thank you for giving me a different kid, it wasn't the first time you said it or the second time, but every time I heard you, you were consistent. I said, thank you. She goes, my name is Sandra, do you want to talk about me on TV? Thank you, Sandra. I've never forgotten Sandra, that was some time in the nineties. I went home, I thought about that story. I still think about that story.

I think about that story because that to me is the definition of what a brand is, that's when I shifted.

A brand says I can depend on you. I can depend on your product, I can depend on what you have to offer. I trust that what you have to offer me is going to serve me well. Okay, I accept that, I'm a brand. Why? Because I believe in the power of consistency and a brand is consistency over time, so I accept it. Yes, I'm a brand now. How did that happen? How did that really happen? You know from the very beginning of my television career and the talk show business, I intuitively used my intuition as my guide and I intuitively understood that the mission of the show, which was my business. That the mission of the show was actually bigger than the show itself.

When I did the very first national Oprah Winfrey Show, I said on air, our mission and vision here is to let people know that they are not alone. When I started in television, I was 19 years old. I was just really happy to just have a job.

I was in Nashville, at this time I was making $20,000 a year. I moved to Baltimore, I was making $22,000 a year when I was 22. And my girlfriend Gayle at the time whom I met in the newsroom, my best friend Gayle said, 'oh, my God! You're 22 and you're making 22, imagine if you're 30, you're making 30! Then you're 40 and you're making 40, oh my God! I made every salary, 22, 25, 27, 30, 35 all the way to $225,000 when I came to Chicago, dropped the mic. I said Oprah, it's over, I'm done. That's it, I don't need to make any more money. The little-known fact is that before I came to Chicago, I did a show in Baltimore called 'People are Talking.' That show had been syndicated. I did that show with a guy named Richard Sher. We were syndicated and a little-known fact is, we were syndicated in about 20 cities and my Westinghouse contact at the time said that if I got to a hundred cities, I would make an extra 10,000. I'm so glad that deal did not go through.

So, when I came to Chicago, I started doing this local talk show. It was a small little business, it was me and four other producers in the room, I say five producers and a gay guy. We were in the room, we did everything, we booked, we did the limo service. We got the guests, I would call up the guests. I would end up losing guests because I only believed in telling the truth to the guests. I remember they put me on the phone once to get Marina Oswald, who was Lee Harvey Oswald's wife, and they wanted her to come on the show. They put me on the phone to tell her to come on the show and I get on the phone, and she says, 'I'm just really worried that if I come on the show, people are going to recognize me.' I go, oh, they will, they're going to recognize you. You won't be able to go to the grocery store anymore, you should probably not even do this. If you worried about people recognizing you, this is not the place to come.

I would lose guests, so they took me off of booking and I became the person that would go out and get lunch for everybody. Taco Bell today, Wendy's tomorrow. So, we have this little family office until we became a syndicated show. Now, the interesting thing is I knew from the beginning that the show, I felt inside myself intuitively that the show would be successful nationally. The reason I believe that is I received a letter from a woman in Ann Arbor, Michigan named Carol. Carol said, 'Watching you be yourself every day makes me want to be more of myself.' I had that letter framed in my office for a very long time. I had that letter framed because that is the moment that I realized that this was more than just a show.

We're being able to reach people in such a way that somebody sees me and doesn't say, I want to be like you. They say watching you makes me want to be more like me, that's big. That's real connection. Carol in Ann Arbor, Michigan allowed me to see and know that we were doing what all business wants to do, and that is to connect to the customer, our customer was, of course, the audience. We were successful as a talk show from day one, out of the box beating Phil Donahue. That was the station's number one goal was to beat Phil Donahue. They didn't think that was possible, when I came to Chicago, they said, you're not going to be able to beat Donahue. You're not going to be able to do that. He's the King of Talk, you're not going to be able to do it.

Here's the keyword, just be yourself. I said, okay that's good, cause I can't be Phil Donahue. I'm the only person I know how to be. I was really happy doing this show that seems to work and all the management was pleased, and everything was working, and things were going well. Then came this moment that changed everything.

OPRAH WINFREY

[Showing an excerpt from a show with a skinhead guest]

-You just said I don't sit with monkeys. You think because she's black because I'm black, we're monkeys?

-That's a proven fact.

-That's a proven fact? It's a proven fact that I'm a monkey?

-Could be.

So that was a show with the skinheads and the KKK. I was doing that show because I thought we were going to expose them for their vitriol, and we would talk about how they mistreated people, and everybody would get to see them for who they really are. During this commercial break, right after that incident of the monkey business, I saw them signaling each other in the audience. I thought, whoa what's going on there? They're giving each other hand signals and whispering and so forth. I realized something came over me again, feeling of instinct, intuition. Wow! These guys are using me. These guys are using me, they are using this platform. I am being used: I think I'm using them, but they are using me. I finished that show, and I made a decision. I went to the producers, and I said, never again. Never again, am I doing a show with the clan or the skinheads or anything that represents the dark side or evil or anything that is going to negatively affect the audience. I'll never be used for somebody else's agenda again.

I said we're not doing the negative stuff. They (producers) go, well, what are we going to do? Keyword here, decision. I felt it so strongly inside myself that I thought if I cannot use this platform, because that's what it is. If I cannot use this platform as a force for something that's positive and good, I will get out of the business. I will figure out something else to do because I cannot be a part of that energy. The decision to change the way I saw television, to begin to use television and not let television use me, was the paradigm shift that allowed the show to take off. There's a quote by Goethe that says, 'Concerning all acts of initiative and creation, there is one elementary truth, that ignorance of which kills countless ideas and splendid plans.' This is the key, that the moment one definitely commits oneself, then providence moves too.

The moment you decide, a whole stream of events, a whole suite of issues from this decision, raising in one's favor all manner of unforeseen incidents and meetings and material assistance, which no man could have dreamed would come his way. Once you make a decision, the energy of the universe rises up to meet you exactly where you are, to help you with providence to move forward. It was the decision, the decision that everybody at some point in time in their business, in their relationship has to make. That was a paradigm shift that propelled me forward. Around the same time as providence would have it, I read this book by Gary Zukav, the book is called the Seat of the Soul. It's 1989 and in this book, he talks about the principle of intention, and he says that every action, thought and feeling. Hear me now, is motivated by an intention.

Every action, everything you do, everything you think is motivated by an intention and that intention is at one with cause and effect, it exists as one. Which means you can't participate in the cause and not participate in the effect. In this most profound way, he says we are held responsible for every action, thought and feeling and therefore our intention. My life, my entire life, my business, my relationships were never the same once I actually understood. Not just read it, not just talked about it, but understood and lived this principle of intention. This is what has defined my life and my business and to fully understand intention, you have to understand how it moves in your life. The vehicle for intention is actually the law of cause and effect. Some people call that law karma, in our country we say, do unto others, as you would have them do unto you.

Well, intention is not just a principle, it actually is law. It's a force that acts as one with a cause and effect or karma. It's also called the third law of motion in physics which says this, for every action there is an equal and opposite reaction. What goes around bam! Comes around. What you put out is coming back. Bam! All the time. Bam! Whether you believe it or not, it's happening. The energy of your intention causes the effect or outcome in every single section. Bam! That is happening, it's not a belief, it's a law. I did a movie called The Color Purple, and the character Sealy, played by Whoopi Goldberg, said it best. This is the law.

[Playing an Excerpt from The Color Purple]

Everything you done to me, already done to you.

Wow! That is happening all the time in your life whether you know it or not. Everything you think and everything you do energetically is coming back to you. Now, I used to hear this all the time about doing unto others as you'd have them do unto you and I'd be like, well, I don't care if he talks about me because I'm talking about her. Its' okay. That's not how it works, the same person that you're doing something to, doesn't have to do something to you. It's the energy of the gossip, it's the energy of the negativity. It's the energy of the intention that is going to come back to you because intention is everything. This changed the way I operated my entire life, so I don't do anything unless it's intentional. Being here with you today, I'm here because I wanted to be here. I'm here because whatever it is I might say, my intention is to leave you with some piece of light that enters your heart space, in a way that you leave here feeling more deserving and more willing to step into your own power.

Now, the truth is the first guests I tried this with, I won my first Emmy. I was like, whoa! That was effective. I wasn't trying to win an Emmy, I was really just excavating the truth for myself. What happened was, it was so powerful that I started doing it for every show. I used to not go into the green rooms because I didn't want to talk to people before the show, I wanted them to be completely spontaneous on the air. For shows that were particularly critical or were going to cause somebody to feel a sense of sadness or remorse, I would go in, and I would meet the people to try to make them feel more comfortable and to talk about what the process would be. But after I discovered this principle of intention, I would go into the green rooms, and I would say it to the guests. The first woman I said this, was on the show because her 16-year-old daughter had been murdered by her 16-year-old boyfriend. Because domestic violence among teenagers is as high as it is with grown women.

This beautiful blonde 16 year old had been murdered by her boyfriend. The mother and father had no idea that the boyfriend was abusing their daughter, Brittany. When I asked the mother, please tell me why you're here. She said, 'I'm here because your producers asked me to be here.' I said no, but why did you actually come? What is your motivation and your intention for being here? She said, I want people to know that Brittany's life was bigger than her death. Everywhere I go, people talk about the murder, but her life was bigger than the murder. I want people to know that she was a girl who loved us. She loved her family, she loved her sisters. Her friends loved her, she laughed, she did things, she played the violin, she wanted to go to music school. I said okay, that's your intention to let people know that your daughter's life was bigger than her death. I can do that cause I control the microphone. Now let me tell you what my intention is.

My intention is to exploit your daughter's life, for the purpose of letting every other 16-year-old, 14 years old, 15 years old,

12 years old, 40 years old, who is in the same situation as Brittany and hiding it, letting them know there is a way out. My intention is to use your daughter's life in such a way that other people can see themselves in her and be lifted from their own despair, sorrow, pain, dysfunction, and secrets. That's my intention. Every question that I ask you, is not me being a voyeur, but it's me trying to excavate the truth, so that other people can see themselves in your daughter's story. It was one of the best interviews I'd ever done and changed the way I did interviews. Whitney Houston on our show in 2007, before we did the whole greeting. Hey girl, how you doing? I said stop the tape, stop the tape. Let's go behind the curtain, tell me why you're really here. What is your intention?

Just recently I was interviewing for Super Soul Sunday, my favorite show on OWN. Thank you very much, you'll see this interview coming up. A young man named Shaka Senghor, 19 years old sentenced to 19 years of prison with second-degree murder. Seven and a half years in solitary confinement and released five years ago. He's now 43, he's written a book called 'Writing my Wrongs.' I said to him before the show, tell me Shaka, what's your intention. He says, I want people to know that you're not the biggest mistake you've ever made. I want people to know redemption is possible. I said okay, I can do that, here's my intention. My intention is you big, you black, you got dreadlocks. You got tattoos, you got 19-year prison sentence behind you. When I introduce you, people are going to see that, they're going to hear that, they're going to feel that. My intention is to humanize you so that people won't see the package, but they will be able to feel what's inside.

Twenty minutes in that interview, that big black man started to cry because I asked him the question, how did you end up on the streets? A question he didn't even know the answer to. I've read his book and I said, I think you ended up on the streets because you always wanted to be a doctor. There was a moment in your story where you came home as a nine-year-old boy, you remember that moment? He said yes, I remember that moment. The moment you came home as a nine-year-old boy, and you had all A's on your report card, and you walked in, and your mother threw a pot of spaghetti at you and cracked the tiles on the walls. You walked out, cleaned up yourself, though, what did I do that for? Why did I work so hard? I think that's the moment. That was the moment you decided not worth it to keep trying in this family. My intention to humanize him, I wasn't trying to make him cry. I was trying to make him feel.

My intention with all of my work is to try to use the ability to connect to other people, to open the heart space. That's why we were number one for 25 years, because our programming was intentionally conceived and designed to do exactly what we did. Never again. Never again I said am I going to be used for somebody else's agenda. What is my agenda? It shifted from just being a talk show to recognizing the power of the platform and recognizing that I am an energetic force. In everything that I'm putting out into the world is an energetic force, your business is an energetic force in the world. Your life is an energetic force field in the world, and it is required of you as a human on the planet, getting along with other humans on the planet, to be responsible for the energy that you are putting into the world.

I interviewed Jill Bolte Taylor, a neuroscientist who had a stroke, wrote a beautiful book called My Stroke of Insight. She couldn't speak, couldn't talk, couldn't feed herself, didn't know numbers, anything. After she had a stroke, now she's back to normal. But she said when she was in that state, she had a sign made that said, to all the people coming into the room, because it was a stroke in the right part of her brain. Left part of her brain, only the right part of her brain was working. She could feel the energy of people there coming into the room. She could feel when the nurses were coming into the room, and they were already thinking about wanting to get out. She could feel when somebody put a plate down for her and they were thoughtful enough to recognize that she couldn't pick up the spoon and would help her with the spoon. She could feel the energy of that.

So, she put a sign outside her door that I actually copied and put in my makeup room, 'Be responsible for the energy that you bring into this room.' Because your energy is literally vibrational, and you have to have good vibrations about your business and your life. The reason why I've been able to do as well as I've done is because I understand it's all the same. It's all the same. No matter how hard you try to balance it, you can't separate the two because your true work on earth, no matter what you choose, your true work on earth is what you've been called to do in some form or another and your true work on earth is your offering. It's the way you express yourself in service to the world. Your fullest, highest expression comes obviously when you do what you love. When you do what you love and you have a passion for, obviously a spark for, when you are doing something that allows you to fill your juice, when you do actually what you came here to do.

One of the reasons why that show, you just couldn't beat us. You just could not beat us because I was doing exactly what I was supposed to do at the time. Why? Because of this from Gary Zukav; 'When your personality comes to serve the energy of your soul, that is authentic empowerment.' I want to say it again, when you can take your personality which we all have, and I got a big one. When you can use your personality to serve that which is deeper, wider, stronger, higher than you can ever imagine. When you align the energy of your personality with what your soul actually came here to do, nobody can touch you. Nobody is as good at doing what you are supposed to do as you, when you are in alignment.

So, my intention became to do exactly what you all are doing here, is to serve the audience, the customer, and to serve the mission, clarifying even deeper what it means to be a force for good. It's one thing to say, I want to be a force for good, but what's our mission? So, every single day, for every single day since 1989, when I read that book. The producers would come in with lists and lists, so you can imagine every day there's just more and more stuff, more subjects every day. It doesn't matter how good a job you do on Tuesday, because Wednesday is another day. You have that feeling? Another day, another show. But every single day up until the very last show, I had a pre-show meeting. I did two shows a day and I had a post-show meeting to see if we fulfill the intention that we said we were going to fulfill. I would ask every producer before they brought me the idea, state the intention at the top and be very clear. State what is your motivation and your intention for doing the show.

Our mission was to uplift, to enlighten, to encourage, to inform and entertain. Some days it's just entertaining. Hi, Chris Rock. Hey, Oprah. Some days, the producers they're booking Brad Pitt and they're going, it's Brad Pitt why do I need an intention? I go I need an intention to sit in the seat, they say just look at him! Just look at him. So, every show's intention, so sometimes I say okay, the intention is let's look at Brad Pitt and dream. Every show's intention was to serve that for the audience and my leadership with our teams reinforced it. Tell me what is your intention? What is your intention? It's a difference, it's like being a florist, some florists sell flowers, some sell beauty. Some sell flowers, some sell celebration. Some sell flowers, some sell creativity. When you can look to whatever it is, you have chosen as your vehicle of expressing yourself on the planet and shift the paradigm to service, everything changes. Service.

Every company represented here today is in service to its public. I think that the greatest calling really, other than being a good mother or father, which is also in service to your children, the greatest calling is service. Martin Luther king said it better than I when he said; 'Not everybody can be famous, but everybody can be great because greatness is determined by service.' Once I discovered this power of intention which influenced my life so greatly, my number one question for every show was how does this serve our audience? Now intention changed my life because I used to be a pleaser, I know a lot of women are. I used to be one of those people who could never say no and then I'd say yes, and then I'd resent you for it. Then you call me again and I'd be upset because I couldn't understand because I already did that once. Now you are calling me back why are you calling me back?

The reason they're calling you back is because when your intention is to please people, you do. When your intention is to make them think you're a nice, oh, make them think call me when nobody else will serve you. Call me when you need somebody to pick up your kids for the fifth time this month. Call me cause I don't want to say no to you, then they do. I learned that the reason why people keep coming back is because I'm not clear about my intention. The question is how will you serve? How do you use that which is yourself and is of your business, to fulfill the highest expression for yourself and your business, that is possible for you. Well, in anybody's business, you're going to make mistakes and my feeling is don't make worthless mistakes. Let every mistake move you forward.

I'm asking the same question now of the OWN network. My biggest mistake when I started the network was assuming that I was speaking to the same audience that I knew for 25 years. Cause I grew up with that audience and everybody grew up with me and their kids came home from school and watched the Oprah Show. I raised a bunch of y'all, I did. I did a good job too I can see that I did a good job. The Oprah Show was a habit. My biggest mistake was not recognizing that that was a habit and now I've got to create another habit over here on the network. The biggest question I ask all the time is, now how can we serve this audience? Cause this isn't the same audience that I grew up with for 25 years. It took us a minute, minute and two years, to find our footing.

I got to tell you, it felt terrible. I was embarrassed being labeled a struggling network. Everywhere I turned, because all of my mistakes ended up either on the CNN crawl or the evening news. But I'd learned something back in 1998, that served me well when I was going through the trial of starting from scratch to build a network, show by show by show. I was on trial in 1998 for saying something bad about a burger. For six weeks, I was in the courtroom every single day for saying something bad about a burger. I said stop me cold from eating another burger over mad cow disease. The cattlemen sued me, and I was literally in a courtroom every day. What I realized when I was in the courtroom every day, is that everybody has trials. There's not a person in this room who's over 17, who hadn't had some trials. Because I have such a big, magnified life, I get to have a real trial with a judge.

What I learned during the trial is to ask this question, what is it here to teach me? Because there is not one thing that is happening in your life that isn't there to give you information about how to move to the next level. Everything is there, everything is there. So, I asked the question, what is this here? What is this here to teach me? That's where I met Dr. Phil, he goes, these good old boys going to hand you your ass on a platter girl. You keep asking that question. They just want to know why you said what you said. But I said, there's a bigger thing going on, what is this here to teach me? What am I blind to that I'm not seeing? Why is that trial is in your face for? How can I use this to move myself forward? Trial builds strength. The other question I ask is, what is my role in it? What did I do to get here?

What I learned about that trial was, obviously I wasn't trying to take the cattle industry down, but it gave me respect for what I said, and how I said it. It pulled me up, it made me recognize, and in an even more magnificent way, what it means to have a platform that speaks to millions of people every day. You have to be careful of what you say and how you say it. Even a trial, all mistakes, this is what I know, no experience is wasted. Everything that has ever happened to you has also happened for you. I look back at all the mistakes that I made when I was building this network and I can see now, oh, that was there to show me. That was there to show me, that was there to humble me. When everybody was writing me off and saying, Oprah you should have kept your day job.

Everywhere I turned, I could hear it in the press. I stopped listening to the press, to other people's opinions. To what everybody else had to say about what I should be doing. I got real still. I got real still, because this is what I learned from Maya Angelou. The voices of the world will drown out your instinct, will drown out the voice of God. Will drown out that what is pure and true to you if you can't get still enough to know for yourself what direction to move. When you don't know what to do, I've learned, do nothing until you do. The voices of the world will drown out that still, small voice of intuition if you let it. I said God listen, you're the one that brought David Zasloff to me, with this idea for a network. If you want me to do this thing, then you got to show me a way. Two days later, Tyler Perry called and said, let me help you. I got an idea for a drama series, Have and Have-Nots.

He brought the first scripted drama to OWN and now we're in the scripted business with many other producers. Craig Wright, who did Lost and Six Feet Under. Ava DuVernay who did Selma. We turned it around. We turned it around using the principle of cause and effect. Using the principle of intention, using the principle of consistency in making the next right move. Sometimes you get so overwhelmed, you just don't know what is the next thing to do, as we were. Biggest mistake

I made, biggest, biggest mistake I made was starting a network while still trying to end the show and not having the right leadership. Anybody in here who has tried to get other people to come in and do what you knew needed to be done, and they were the wrong people, you know without the right leadership, you can go nowhere.

That was my biggest mistake. Another mistake is not paying attention to all the whispers that were showing up. You know I have 185 daughters in college that I'm paying for: 185, 20 in the United States and the rest in South Africa. I was Face Timing yesterday with one of my daughters, who's at Brown University she's a junior and she's telling me how overwhelming the junior year is. How stressful it is, and how I just can't believe all the things that she has to do, because I mean, my God, I'm a junior Mamo! I said what's the next right move? Let's just go through this right now on the phone. What is the next right move? Well, I got four papers to turn in. I go, which one are you going to turn in first, because you can't do them all at the same time. What is the next right move?

Building a great business is really like for me, building a great life. You learn from your mistakes, which creates strength. You let what looks like failure be your greatest teacher. I say that to my girls all the time. I was talking to Scott backstage, you pay attention to the whispers because this is what shows up. Whispers show up in your life all the time, trying to provide a message for you to move in another direction and many people don't get the whispers. What I've learned is, if you don't pay attention to the whispers, they turn into little pebbles, and it gets harder and louder. Pebbles usually represent a problem has shown up, because you didn't pay attention when the whisper showed up. If you don't pay attention to the pebble, the brick is coming.

A lot of brick people, the brick is coming and the brick is now, when you could have gotten it in the message, now you in a full-blown crisis because you didn't do anything when you had a problem and when you got the message, and if you don't handle the crisis, you end up with a full-blown disaster on your head. I teach that to my girls, I also constantly remind myself and I say to the universe, I say to God, I say to life, let me get it in the whisper, don't teach me nothing new today. Messages unheeded turn into problems like pebbles and crisis into disaster. What I say to you, what I'm constantly reminding myself, is to pay attention to your life because your life is speaking to you always in all ways. Even when situations look beyond your control, you actually have the power to shift the way you think about it. You can shift the way you see things and things begin to be seen differently. So, when OWN and I were getting bashed on a daily basis.

[Excerpt from News Report about OWN] 15 months after OWN's heralded debut, headlines around the country warn that Winfrey's daring TV adventure is in trouble. So how did the number one woman in TV end up like this?

I don't know. I don't know. But when I was seeing all those stories, I had to say to myself, okay, what is this here to teach me? I must need to learn a whole lot. Also, I asked how can I see it differently? What is being reflected to me is actually the struggles, anytime anybody asked me about it, I go, oh, it's a struggle. It's a struggle honey. Oh, network is a struggle. It's a struggle, because my life is so big, that's what was being reflected back to me in the news. Every time anybody talked about it and said, it's a struggle, it's a struggle. Then I'd say, oh yes, it's a struggle. So much a struggle! Climbing up a mountain, it's a struggle. One day. I had one of those come to a Jesus meetings with myself under the oaks and say, show me another way. I realized I needed to do what I'm sure at some point you might need to do, need to change the narrative. Need to change the narrative for myself, the story that I was telling myself about myself, for what myself could accomplish.

You need to change the narrative. How can I see it differently? Because everything comes back to the truth of you and me. What is the truth? What are you really here on the planet to serve? All of the businesses, all of the work, all of the long hours, all of the commitment, all of the dedication, all the devotion, all of that is about what really, are you here to serve? That's bigger than your business, you use your business as a vehicle, as a tool of expressing who you choose to be on the planet. But what is the real calling? Why are you really here? What is the real work to be done? How do you open yourself up to feel and express and know that, in the fullest, most powerful way?

Again, I say your work and life are not separate. Your work is your vehicle for your truest expression and one of the reasons why the show was like a heart, open heart feel for me. It was just like feeling hearts every day, because I understand that although I have made more money than I ever imagined, the money isn't what makes me.

Although I have seen and done and accomplished more than I ever dreamed of as a poor little girl growing up in Kosciusko, Mississippi. I still have my feet on the ground, though I'm wearing better shoes. I understand that there really is no difference in separation between what people think is famous, because fame by definition, is just that more people know your name and ask for selfies. I would just like to make a national request, the next person please know how to work your own phone. I love all these old people, my age, we want to do a selfie and they're like what? What? Where? Turn the camera on ma'am, turn it on. Oh, selfies have changed the world. This is what I know, though, this is what I know that you want the same thing I want, it may come in a different package. It may look different, your square footage may be different. Your car may be different. I have a new Tesla, it's too fast for me. I'm going to go back to my bug cause I just can't handle it.

We have differences of what makes us feel valued and worthy in the world. But when it comes down to it, you want the same thing I want, that is to be able to live out the truest, highest, expression of yourself as a human being and to use your work to be an expression of your highest offering to the planet. I wish you joy in that. I wish you the best of intention in that, because you're being here in this room today is no fluke. It is no accident, it is no luck. There is no lucky without a lot of preparation meeting the moment of opportunity. And just the fact that you are here, and you have worked, and you have tried. You have sometimes failed, and you have been challenged and you kept getting up and you didn't turn away and you didn't turn back. You knew that there was something greater ahead for you and you used those moments to build strength.

Every time it looked like you weren't going to be able to make payroll, you used those moments to create a sense of determination. This is what I know, strength, time strength equals power. Everybody in here, there's a level of consciousness of work. You're waiting on the big moment, the big break, will you be the winner to get your Super Bowl commercial. Waiting on the big moment, I wish it could be all of you. You're waiting on the moment and I'm telling you, the moments are waiting for you. I want you to leave here and make a decision to step into your power and watch what happens. Bam! Bam! What you are putting out? Bam! Is coming back. Thank you.

OPRAH WINFREY

Harry's Last Lecture at Stanford University
(2015)

Hi you all. You all just don't even know, what does it mean to me to be standing in this hall. In 1970, before you were even a thought, in the mind of God or in the seed of your parents, I was in an oratorical contest as a junior at East High School. The great victory for us as state champions was to have our national championship here at Stanford, in this very church. As I stand here today, I lost the contest, but I won the prize. Wow! I know I came in today and I went, oh my gosh, I made it!

Dean Shaw, that introduction moves me, because one of my goals as a human being has been to evolve to the point of being a student in the spiritual realm. Enough that I could be able to bestow some of my knowledge, the information I've gathered over the years from thousands of interviews, in such a way that I could call myself a teacher. I dared to not call myself a teacher until hearing it from you and because you have said I'm a teacher and you are here at Stanford, I believe you, I'm going to take that. So thank you.

It's been an amazing day here with you all. First of all. I have one of my South African daughters, I have 20 girls in college, in the United States, and one of them Chaday, is here at Stanford. She's a sophomore and we came to Stanford, I think late 2011 or early 2012, I can't remember. I remember landing on the campus with her and we didn't know if she was going to get in yet. As we got into the car and we're pulling away, she said, Mamo, these are my people. I can understand why, just being here in the presence of such energetic, stimulated brilliance makes us all want to be better. I wish I could have gone to this school. I'm thrilled that I have one of my daughters who does go to this school. I love everything that happens here in the bubble.

I'm really excited to be a part of the Harry Rockburne Lecture Series, because I have spent hundreds and hundreds and hundreds and thousands of hours talking to spiritual leaders and teachers. Not just spiritual leaders and teachers who have been deemed so, but thousands of people who came from levels of dysfunction. Who came from levels of pain, who were suffering, who were challenged in their progression of trying to be the best human beings they could be. They allowed themselves the opportunity to come on our show, the Oprah Winfrey Show and share their stories. I am one who believes in the sharing of stories. I believe in the process of sharing period, because I know that all life gets better when you share it. Those thousands of people who have been guests on the show, and many of them who are also audience members have been my greatest teachers. I would say that one of my gifts and it's everybody's job to know what your gift is. When I talk about my gift, I'm not bragging it's just fact. It's just a fact, it's a gift yes.

One of my gifts that I've had since I was a little girl growing up in Mississippi, being raised on a tiny, little acre farm with my grandmother is that I knew how to pay attention. I was a great observer of life, and I grew up believing that I was indeed for sure God's child. It's because every Sunday I sat in our little church down the road, a dirt road from where my grandmother lived. No running water, no electricity. I was saying this to my great-niece who's eight the other day. She said, it sounds like Little House on the Prairie, and I go, it kind of was. No running water, no electricity, but the church is down the road from us, and we could hear the singing as I was getting dressed for Sunday school. I'd always sit on the left-hand side, the left pew in the second row. I would listen to the preacher, preach about the Lord thy God is a loving God. Sometimes he would say the Lord that God is a jealous God. But most important, I heard him say you are God's child and through God all things are possible.

I literally took him at his word so that by the time I had to leave my grandmother, because she became ill and I was sent to live in Milwaukee with my mother, who had two other children. I got beat up on the playground, because when people would ask me, who is your daddy, I would say Jesus, is my daddy. Sometimes he's my brother and God is my father. But what I now know and have learned that my view of God, although I call that God in a box and although that my vision of God has expanded to be inclusive of all things all. God is all, God is law. God is all, in all things. Not just the guy standing up and sitting up with the beard. Now that view of God has expanded, I still understand how important it was for a little colored girl. We weren't even black yet, not to mention African American, you know what I mean, Harry.

A little colored girl in Mississippi for whom there was no vision of hope or possibility. My grandmother's greatest desire for me as she had been a maid and her mother before her had been a maid. Her greatest desire was that I would grow up one day and be able to do the same. She wished for me that I would be able to, she used to say, I hope you get some good white folks when you grow up. I hope you get good white folks who treat you good.

So my grandmother would have no idea of the life that I now lead with good white folks who are working for me, she just wouldn't get it. She wouldn't get it, but somehow I think she must know and she's up around in the spirit realm saying, Lord have mercy, I didn't see it. But I now know that having that belief system, that something greater than me was in charge of my destiny, of my fate, that it wasn't just me alone having to survive for myself, is the thing, is the value, is the rock that has sustained me. My vision, my perception, my understanding of what it means to be a universal citizen has grown. As I came to understand Acts 17:28, my favorite Bible verse that says, 'In God I move and breathe and have my being.' So my every attempt in life has been since I was a little girl, to be in that space that I call God. To literally live in the breath that is God. To live in the breath and allow the breath to breathe me as God.

That is the reason I see, I have been able to manage fame, handle the success, grow in grace, grow in the wisdom and glory that is offered by that space that I know to be God. Because in God, I live in breathe. I move and breathe, and I have my being. In everything that I do and all that I am, comes up and out from the center of that space, even when I didn't know what to call it. I have paid attention to my life because I understand that my life just like your life is always speaking to you. Where you are, in the language, with the people, with the circumstances and experiences that you can understand and interpret if you are willing to see that always life, God is speaking to you. Now it took me a while to actually really get this and to understand it, but once I did, I started paying attention to everything. One of the reasons why I can now accept the fact that I can offer my gatherings of information and wisdom and call myself a spiritual teacher, is that every single person who ever came on my show and I hear there was like 37,000 guests I've talked to.

A lot of them came from dysfunction and a lot of them wouldn't appear to be teachers, but every one of them had something to say that was meaningful and valuable and that I could use to grow myself into the best of myself, which is what all of our jobs are. Your number one job is to become more of yourself and to grow yourself into the best of you. So I had a lot of great teachers, as we all do. I mean old boyfriends are some of the best teachers. Woo boy! I got a doctorate degree for one, I'll tell you about that later. But I was doing an Oprah show about a decade ago. One of my greatest teachers was a man named John Diaz. We were doing a show called, Would you Survive? And on Tuesday, October 31, 2000, Singapore Airlines Flight 006, a Boeing 747 from Taipei to Los Angeles, took off with 179 souls aboard. Four crew and 79 passengers perished in that flight, a total of 83 fatalities. There was a typhoon rolling through at the time and the plane went down the wrong runway.

Now what's interesting, john Diaz was on that plane and he had had several, several indications, which I'll talk about later. Whispers that he shouldn't have gotten on the plane, but he did anyway. He got on the plane, and he managed to be one of the survivors and on the Oprah show, I was asking him what do you think it was that you were the one of the survivors? I said do you think it was your position on the plane? Cause he was in first class, and he was sitting on the right next to an exit door and he said yes, I think it might've been the position of the plane and also my quick thinking, he says, and the fact that I didn't stop moving. I said you don't believe you're not a religious man. You don't believe that there was some kind of divine intervention going on there? He goes, no, I'm not a religious person. I do not believe that it was anything divine, I don't believe that. I did see he said, as I got knocked back into the plane, that it looked like Dante's Inferno, with people strapped into their seats and just burning.

It seemed a bit to me, as I turned and looked backwards, like there was a light coming out of the top of their heads. I guess you could call it an aura, was leaving their bodies and some lights were brighter than others. It changed he said, it changed me, it gave me a new kind of spirituality in a sense that I now believe somehow, I don't know how, but life continues on somehow through that light. I thought, you know, I'm not a religious man, but I thought the brightness and dimness of the auras were how one lives one's life so to speak. So that's one of the major things that really has changed with me since then, he says. I want to live my life so my aura when it leaves is one of the brightest ones. I got chills when he said that so much so, nothing to do but go to a commercial, we'll be right back. What do you say after that? I want to live my life, so when my aura leaves, it's very bright. That's one of those moments that happens, and you know that it's bigger than a show about survivors.

Because I always knew that when I am moved, at least a million other people might be too, because if I can feel it and there are 20 million people watching around the world, it means that somebody else also felt and heard the same thing. That's what connection is. I thought a lot about that and thought about it, obviously in thinking about, in preparing to talk to you all today about how does one lead a meaningful life? Because ultimately isn't that what we all want. We want to lead a life so that however we transition, people can say, wow! That was a bright one. That was a bright light. First of all, I think that it comes from a deep sense of awareness about who you are and why you're here. It comes from being in touch with, on a regular basis, the appreciation and the holy gratitude that should fill each of our hearts on a regular basis. Just knowing what a privilege it is to be here and to be human.

Close your eyes for a moment, will you please? Breathe with me. Just close your eyes and if you will ,put your thumb to your middle finger and gather your other fingers around and let's feel the vibration and pulse of your personal energy as you take three deep breaths with me. Inhale and as you exhale, just feel the vibration, energy, blood pulsating through your body, through you. Another inhale. Ah! Another inhale and keep your eyes closed. Let's just think about this day, this day that you have been graced to breathe in and out thousands of times. This day, where many of those breaths were taken for granted, you just expected the next one to come. But the truth is there's no guarantee that the next one comes. This day, how you started your day, what your thoughts were this morning. How you've carried yourself through this day. How you've been allowed to have encounters and experiences, some challenging, some more life enhancing that pushed you forward another day of being here on the planet earth as a human being.

Let's just think about that, after all you've been through in this day alone, and the many days and years past. How you got here to this prestigious esteemed university, the choices you made that have brought you to this day. Open your heart and quietly to yourself, say the only prayer that's ever needed. Thank you. Thank you. Thank you. You're still here and you get another chance this day to do better and be better. Another chance to become more of who you were created and what you were created to fulfill. Thank you. Amen. Open your eyes. That's how it starts, that is the foundation for meaning and purpose in your life. It is to bring yourself back to your breath in all situations, in all ways, and all challenges to know that the value of just still being here matters. It's really big that you're here, it's really big because everybody here has been called from the ethers to do the will, to fulfill the highest expression of yourself as a human being and to do that in truth.

How do you do that? Well, I think you let every step you take move you in the direction of the one thing all religions can agree on, and that is love. In all the conversations I've had with so many people over the years, who run the gamut of all kinds of emotions and emotional dysfunction. I've come to understand that what Marianne Williamson said is true, there's really only two emotions that count and that's love and that's fear. In all of your movements through life, you're either moving in the direction of one or the other. In order to have a meaningful life, you have to choose love and not the schmaltzy doltzy kind of love, but the kind of love that really counts. The kind of love that when everything else is going wrong and nobody even knows you're choosing it, you choose love. The kind of love that says I'm here for you no matter what, you choose love. The kind of love that means you make the right decision even when you know the other person is wrong.

You choose love because love is not just, it's a verb and it's everything that represents kindness and grace and harmony and cooperation and reverence for life. So when you choose, when you're in a situation where you are mad, you are mad, and you know they are wrong. If you can go to that space of the breath, in God I move and breathe and have my being and make the choice just to move a little closer in the direction of that, which is going to bring you grace. That which is going to honor yourself and by honoring yourself, you can't help but honor the other person. I have learned to choose love over fear, to choose love and peace rather than choosing to be right. That was a big lesson for me. Do you want peace? Do you want love? Do you want to be right? For a little while, I was like, I'd rather be right. Rather be right with a little bit of love. The other thing, you know I am a Christian. I grew up Christian raised in the church all day long on Sundays. Sunday School in the morning, church in the afternoon, Bible School at night. Prayer service Wednesday nights choir practice. I grew up in the church.

I would say I don't go to church as much anymore. My church is nature for me, my church is my life. I experienced church in every encounter with every person, I try to have church. I try to live my life from the tenant of the law, the third law motion in physics. If I had only one wise offering for you, it would be this one. The third law of motion and all the laws of the universe actually are in my mind, divine laws and my favorite is the third law. Which says for every action, there is an equal and opposite reaction. There are lots of different religions and philosophies that call these other things. In this country, sometimes we call it the Golden Rule. What I know for sure is, it doesn't matter what you do unto others, it's already done unto you. So anybody who's seen the movie, The Color Purple, there's a line in there when Ms. Seeley leaves and she says to Mister, everything you done to me and she holds up two fingers, already done to you. That's the third law of motion.

Newton didn't know that Sealy was going to articulate it that way, but everything you done to me, already done to you.

So that is the tenet that rules my entire life and before the third law of motion, which says there's every, every action there's an equal and opposite reaction. Before there's even the thought or the action, there is the intention for the thought. If there is one force field that rules and dominates the meaning of life for me, it is living my life with a pure sense of intention. This came to me because I used to be one of those people who had the disease to please. I said yes many times when I knew I should have been saying no and then I would be mad at myself for saying, yes.

Anybody ever done that? You say yes, then you mad when they come back again. Because when you say yes, when you really mean no, people followed the intention of the yes. Because why do you say yes? You say yes, because you don't want the person to be upset with you. They're not, you don't want the person to be angry, you want the person to think you're nice. They do, and that is why they keep coming back. I couldn't understand. I just gave you some money and now you are back. Oh, that's because I didn't really state the truth and so now you think me giving you the money meant I wanted to give you the money and that's why you're back asking me for some more. I tested this principle of intention when I first came to discover it in Gary Zukav's book Seat of the Soul. I say I'm going to see if that intention thing will work for this disease to please, because people are always bothering me. So this is what I learned through intention, nothing is showing up in your life that you didn't order there. If it's there, it's there because you needed to see it. I have a big life and things show up for me in big ways. One day Stevie Wonder calls me. I'm not name-dropping. It's true, he called me. No brag, just fact. It was Stevie and he didn't call to say he loved me either. He was calling because he wanted something, but that's okay.

I at the time, this was early on, you know cause when I first started making money and it was my salary or my earnings were published all over the place. I mean the first year I was like, really? Did I make that much money? Oh my God! It was very difficult for me to figure out where my boundaries were, because I'd grown up poor and didn't have anything. It's easy when you don't have anything and people ask you for money and they say, I need 500 or say I don't have it cause I'm just trying to get my rent paid. It's harder when your multi-billion-dollar salary is now into paper, and you get a lot of friends and cousins you didn't have before. So how do you set boundaries for yourself? I was having trouble setting boundaries myself for even strangers. People would just show up at my door in Chicago and say, Oprah, I left my husband. Please help me. I would, because she knows I have it. So don't try that now though okay. Don't try that now, I figured it out.

What I learned was is that, oh, the reason why people keep showing up is because my intention is to make them think that I'm such a nice person that you can ask me for anything. You can get me to do anything, I'm going to say yes, I'm going to say yes. When Stevie called me this time, I thought I'd try out my first no on Stevie, let's start big. He wanted me to donate some money to a charity and I didn't want to donate to the charity. Because I have my own charities and I care about a lot of people, but the problem is when you have money, everybody thinks you just want to give to everything. Every letter I ever get starts with, we know you love the children. Yes, I do love the children, but somebody else is going to have to help the children. I said to Stevie no, and as a person who has that disease to please, I was waiting for him then to say, I will never speak to you again. I will never call you. I will never sing a song for you, and he didn't, he just said, okay. Okay? It's okay. He said, okay, check you later.

What I learned from that is many times you will have angst and worry about things and put yourself in a state, like someone said this morning, cause her phone went off. They were mortified over a phone, I said really? You will put yourself in a state when the other person really isn't even thinking about you. So learning that I could specifically determine for myself what the boundaries were for me, what I wanted to do. Give my money, give my time, give of my service to who I wanted to give it to, when I did that, I got to make that decision. Just because you get a hundred requests a week, doesn't mean you have to try to fulfill all of that. Just because you have all of these demands on your time and on you, doesn't mean that you have to say yes. You get to decide because you're the master of your fate. The captain of your soul as William Ernest Henley said in Invictus, and understanding that, really changed the meaning of my life, in that I was no longer driven by what other people wanted me to do. But took charge of my own destiny, making choices based upon what I feel is the next right move for me.

Being able to go continuously to that space that I call the power station of God, universal energy, the divine flow. Being able to tap into the space where you and all of life and me and all of you in this room, all beings, all things are connected. We had a meditation this morning, where we talked about entering that space, that space is real. You cannot, in my opinion, have a meaningful life without a life of self-reflection of spiritual and moral inquiry and knowing who you are and why you are truly here. Spiritual self-reflection, to understand who you are and why you are here. When you understand the depths of that, and you allow yourself to tap into the space of that, which is the force, the universal energy, the divine flow. And you do that with a sense of authenticity that only you can, that only your energy can bring, you become untouchable in whatever it is you choose to do.

So, one of the reasons I believe that I've been able to be so successful is because during the years where we had fierce competition from other shows and other people. I would always say to my producers, you can't run their race, you can only run yours. You really could only run what you're doing. You can't even worry about your own fellow producers. You can only run your own race. That lesson, that Glenda the Good Witch gives to the Wicked Witch of the West, when she says, go away, you have no power here, that's a powerful lesson. Because I have seen over the years in so many interviews and even in my real life experiences, people losing their power because you're giving your power to other people. You lose your power when you try to take control of somebody else's energy, because you have no power in any energy field, other than that which is your own. Your real job in life is to figure out how do you master your field? How do you do that? By consistently choosing love. By living in this space of gratitude and knowing that, that power that you feel from time to time, comes from a source that is greater than yourself.

Because nobody gets out of here alone, nobody. Nobody is making it alone and when you are afraid, when you are sad, when you are unable to make a decision, when you are challenged, when you are moving in the direction of all that which is fearful, it's because you're trusting in your own power. I couldn't get here by my little, bitty ego self. When you look at where I've come from, a little town, apartheid town in Kosciusko, Mississippi. In 1954, where there were more lynchings of black men per capita than any place else in the world. Where you had to be off the streets, literally when white people walk down the street. Where there was no vision or hope for you as a black man or black woman, other than being a domestic or teaching in the colored school. My ability to step into literally the flow and grace that I call God, is what has gotten me. I consistently mind that, because having a spiritual life isn't something that you can attain, because you already are a spiritual life.

Pierre Teilhard de Chardin said, we're spiritual beings having a human experience. I know this to be true. So it's not like you can go out seeking a spiritual life, you already are one and the real job is for you to become aware of the soul's calling and the spirit that resides in above, around and through you, and be about the business of fulfilling that.

There is no one else in creation like you, there's nobody like you. What you've come to do, and what you have to offer is like no other, even if they're all doing the same thing. I met a bunch of people majoring in the Human Biology, I go, Ooh, a lot of human biologists coming out of Stanford, a lot of great ones. Although everybody's in the same class doing very similar things, no one brings the level of uniqueness and authenticity that you can bring, nobody does it like you. Understanding that what you have to offer, what you've come to give to the planet is your gift, your offering in a way that nobody else can and how much that matters. It matters to you, it matters to the people that you love, and it matters to our planet that you are here.

It's a miracle that we get to be here. When I think of my life and the fact that nobody really kind of wanted me in the beginning. My father had sex with my mother one time, can you imagine? I was a powerful seed. Woo. Honey Child! But one time, one time, and he wasn't in love with her. He said she was wearing a poodle skirt and he wanted to know what was up under there and she showed him by an oak tree. Now got a yard full of oaks, I know that's where it all started. To think that something as random as my mother's poodle skirt and my father walking out the door at that time, she'd had her eye on him for a while, so she was working it. To think that something as random as that would create a little Negro child in Mississippi, who grew up and has had, and continues to have the opportunities that I've had, I can assure that is nothing but grace. It's grace, it's grace, because I was allowed to step into the flow of it and let it carry me to this moment.

I'm not telling you what to believe or whom to believe or what to call it, but there is no full life, no fulfilled, meaningful, sustainably, joyful life without a connection to the spirit. I haven't seen it happen and the wait for sustainability is through practice. You must have a spiritual practice. What is yours? Well, for some people, it is going to church and that's where they nurture themselves. I believe that creativity, artful expression, prayer, conscious kindness, empathy, consistent compassion, gratitude, all spiritual practices are the way of becoming more of who you are.

I started a gratitude journal, I mean I was journaling since actually I was standing here in 1970. I actually have in my journal about visiting Stanford and what it meant to come here as an orator. For years, all of my journals were filled with, he didn't love me. I can't believe she did that to me and this is what happened today. About the late eighties, someone introduced the idea of a gratitude journal to me.

Gratitude journaling has become a spiritual practice that leads to a more enhanced and meaningful life, and you can start it today. I guarantee if you did it for a week, you would see a difference. Because every day and I'll do it when I go home, five things I write down that I am grateful for, or that brought me joy or opened my heart space. By practicing gratitude, what you realize is, is that you wake up in the morning thinking about what are those five things going to be? Because some days there's only three and then you have to take a breath, inhale that's one. Exhale, that's two. Okay. I made my five, that's all I got today. Practicing gratitude in a way that allows you to take stock of your life, that's why it's a spiritual practice because you're now taking stock of your life. You're assessing where you are spiritually and in order to maintain a sense of growing yourself forward, it requires also being in a place of knowing that after you've done all that you can. There's a wonderful song by Donnie McClurkin that says, you just stand.

There comes a time in everybody's life when you've actually done all that you can do, and you really want something so badly, but it still isn't coming forward for you in a way that you feel that it should. I know that what is for you will come to you, I know that for sure. I know that many times when it appears that something is happening to you, it is always happening for you. To strengthen you because my definition of power is strength over time, strength, time, strength, time, strength, time, strength...

So I'll leave you with my favorite story. I said this today about The Color Purple. It's one of my favorite stories because it changed the meaning of my life and changed the trajectory of my life. First of all, when I was doing The Color Purple, I just came to Chicago and started a show called AM Chicago, and I'd asked my bosses for the time off. I needed two months to do The Color Purple. They said to me, you don't have two months, your contract says you only get two weeks a year. In order for us to give you the time off, you're going to have to give up your remaining time on your contract to do The Color Purple.

I wanted to do it so badly that I said, all right, I'll give up the next five years of my contract in order to do it. What happened was after The Color Purple, after I filmed The Color Purple and the Oprah Show was so successful, becoming so successful, it was actually still called AM Chicago. The bosses at my channel wanted to renegotiate the contract. My lawyer at the time said, remember The Color Purple. You never want to be in a position where something is that important to you to do, and you can't do it because the boss says you can't. You want to be able to own yourself and make your own decisions about what's important to you to do, and that was something that's really important to you. The fact that I had not been allowed the time for The Color Purple is the reason why I made the decision to take the risk, to own my own show, and that has made all the difference in the trajectory of my career.

But let me try to short this Color Purple story, cause it changed the trajectory of my life. I wanted to be in The Color Purple more than anything I've ever wanted in my life. I read the book on a Sunday. I got up, went back to the bookstore, got every other copy of the book. I passed it out to everybody I knew, I was clearly obsessed about The Color Purple. People see me come and go here she comes talking about The Color Purple. Here she comes again. I literally would walk around with it in a backpack. I see all these backpacks, y'all are loaded down here. I would walk around with it in a backpack in case I ran into somebody who hadn't read it. I'd say, oh, you haven't read it, I have one right here. As life would have it, cause you're always drawing things to you, you're drawing energy to you. Out of nowhere, supposedly, coincidence, no such thing, but I get a call from a casting agent saying that they're casting for this movie called Moon Song and I said, are you sure it's not The Color Purple? No, it's called Moon Song because at the time Steven Spielberg didn't want anybody know he was shooting The Color Purple.

I go and audition for the movie. I can't believe that God has allowed this to happen because I am auditioning with a character named Harpo. Did you all know that Harpo is Oprah spelled backwards? I think that is a direct sign from Jesus. But not only am I now auditioning, I'm auditioning with somebody named Harpo. Amazing!

When all I'd really asked God, I said God, please help me get in this movie. Help me get in this movie. I don't know anybody in the movies. I'm in Chicago doing a show called AM Chicago. I thought I could be a script girl, best girl, best boy whatever, the last credit on the movie. Bottom line is a long time passed, I call up the agent and the agent said you don't call us, we call you and I didn't call you. I hung up the phone, I was so upset. I decided to go to Fat Farm and I'm going to lose the weight, that's what they call them at the time. I'm going to the fat farm, I'm going to starve myself, because now all the weight is caught up with me. I know they hate me because I'm fat I said.

I'm going to go and I'm going to lose weight and I'm going to try to release this obsession that I have with The Color Purple. I'm going to try to let that go, because now much time has passed. I am on the track, running around the track and I can hear my thighs rubbing together and I start crying cause oh gosh! Now my thighs are rubbing together and it's raining, and my hair is getting wet. I started to pray and I'm praying and I'm crying and I'm asking God, actually. God, please help me let this go. I'm obsessed, I want it. Reuben Cannon had told me that real actresses had auditioned for that part and that I wasn't a real actress and that Alfre Woodard had just left his office. I thought for sure, Alfre Woodard is going to get that part. I'm running around the track, praying and crying and the way prayer works is you could pray, but if you don't release it, if you don't surrender it, it goes nowhere. It's just you talking to yourself. So I started singing the song, do you know the song I Surrender All. I surrender all, all to Thee my blessed savior, I surrender all.

I sang and I prayed, and I cried until I could release the pain, the suffering of the rejection that Reuben Cannon had caused me, by telling me that I don't call you. Then I realize, oh, I'm still carrying it around, so I won't be able to go to see the movie. I'm going to now pray that I can bless Alfre Woodard in the movie. Let me bless Alfre Woodard, so I'll be able to go see this movie. I start singing again, I surrender all, please don't let me have now a grudge against Alfre Woodard who took my movie. Let me have peace in my heart about that. So I prayed, I prayed, I prayed until I'm singing I surrender all, a woman comes out and says to me that there's a phone call for you. In that phone call I was told, next day show up in Steven Spielberg's office. If you lose a pound, you could lose this part, so I stopped at the Dairy Queen.

But the point of this story is surrender, and the point of the story is I thought I could just be a script girl, best girl whatever. I was just happy to be anywhere in the film. The point of the story is God can dream, the universe can dream, your creation can dream. The flow of your life can dream, has a bigger plan and a bigger dream for you than you can ever even imagine for yourself. When I finished The Color Purple, Quincy Jones said to me, baby your future is so bright, it burns my eyes. I say the same thing to all of you, you Stanford students with this amazing gift to be at this institution and let your light so shine your brilliance. Your future's so bright, it burns my eyes. The glory that the universe, God has in store for you is unimaginable to you. You can't even imagine it, if you will surrender that which is yourself, in alignment with the greater self, and allow yourself to become a part of the force of all. Take your glory, it's waiting for you and run with it.

Thank you.

Living Brave with Brene Brown
(2016)

Brene: So welcome to Living Brave. Thank you for doing this with me. So these are conversations about courage. With people who I believe are living brave lives, who are inspiring me to be braver and you're one of those people. So thank you,

Oprah: Really?

Brene: We're going to start with a couple of words that are really important to me and really important in my work.

Definition for me, vulnerability is?

Oprah: Being willing to express the truth no matter what. The truth of who you are, the essence at your core of what you're feeling in any given moment. It's being able to open up your soul and let it flow so that other people can see their soul in yours.

Brene: So this is the first question, I'm getting ready to start crying. Give me an example from your life. Give me a specific thing that feels really vulnerable for you still. After all of your experience, what's still vulnerable for you? Not professionally or personally.

Oprah: Weight, discussing weight, not having conquered the whole weight struggle. Figuring out what to eat next, what not to eat. The whole balancing what it means to be a strong, powerful woman in the world, juxtaposed, trying to control what you're eating. Yes, that's still a vulnerable space for me.

Brene: I think when people, you know because we've done work together, people ask me a lot of questions about you, and they tell me the stories they've made up about you.

Oprah: Oh yes, really?

Brene: Yes and I have stories too, but I've gotten to know you a little bit. I know how dangerous stories are that we tell ourselves about ourselves and about other people, especially when we're in comparison. I think people see you as someone who is fearless, who has no more fear, who has conquered all. What do people not know about you in terms of struggle still to be brave? Are there still some struggles you have about being brave with your life?

Oprah: I've worked on the disease to please a lot. As you've heard me say that in 1989, I had a really big breakthrough with that reading Gary Zukav's book on intention. I started literally living an intentional life where I don't make any decisions, unless I think about what is my true, pure motivation for doing it. Because I do recognize the law of cause and effect that says the intention informs even the cause. That before you have an action, there is a reason for you taking that action. The reason for the action is what's going to actually show up in your life on the other end. That's what's going to come back to you, a bad intention. That helped me a lot with the disease to please, because I was always giving. Then I was also thrown when people would come back and ask for more. I couldn't understand why they were asking for more. When people ask for more, because your reason for giving is so that they think that you're nice, that's your real intention. Well, they do think you're nice.

Brene: This is hard to hear, keep going.

Oprah: They do think you're nice and that is why they keep coming back. They come back because you're the nice one you're going to say yes even when you mean no. So you're the person I'm going to call to go pick up my kids when I can't, or don't want to, because you're going to say yes, even if you don't want to do it. That's why people keep coming back when your intention is not really clear. That took a lot of fear away for me, but at least, a clarity of intention helped me live a more fearless life.

Brene: I love that. What if your intention is I want to lead a brave life and not disappoint anyone?

Oprah: You cannot live a brave life without disappointing some people.

Brene: I know that in my heart, but it sounds really important when you say it.

Oprah: You cannot live a brave life without disappointing some people. But those people who get disappointed, it's really okay.

Because the people who really care for you, the people who are rooting for your rise, will not be disappointed. The only people who are disappointed are people who have their own agenda.

Brene: Yes.

Oprah: Their agenda is not aligned with your agenda and that's how I make myself brave. I say, well, the people who really care about you, who are rooting for your rise. Those people who are rooting for your rise, they're going to be okay when you say no.

Brene: Let me ask you this question that's related, very tough in this world that can seem very unforgiving, critical, mean-spirited sometimes even. You shut yourself off from all the feedback and it's dangerous because you need some of it and you need to stay open and connected. But you open yourself up to everything and it will kill you. It will make you less brave because some of it is just not helpful.

Oprah: Right.

Brene: How do you, and I want a really specific answer, how do you stay open to meaningful feedback that can make you better as a leader at what you do? But also filter out the stuff that is just mean-spirited that will hurt you and take you down.

Oprah: Well, first of all, I never read any comments that are coming from negative people. If I start to read something...

Brene: Just shut her down.

Oprah: Shut it down. I will not take that in.

Brene: So how do you open to feedback that is helpful? Are there people you go to? How do you do that?

Oprah: I have a kitchen cabinet since the beginning of my career. Different people have been in that kitchen cabinet over the years, but there are a few people who are my resource, who I know are going to tell me the truth. Steadman is going to tell me the truth, no matter what.

Brene: Hard or even hard truth?

Oprah: The harder, the truther. Bob Green, my friend. Oh my gosh! Brutal sometimes. Bob Green is like my brother. But the reason why we remained friends over the years is he's the only person that's actually been so brutal with the truth, he's made me cry. But he is not afraid to tell me just the brutal truth. I have Bob Green. I have Steadman, I have Gayle who are going to tell me the truth no matter what.

Brene: These are your truth tellers.

Oprah: These are my truth fillers.

Brene: I got a cabinet for sure, and I value them so much because they will tell me what I don't want to hear but need to hear. They'll love me through it, and they'll tell me.

Oprah: This is the other thing your cabinet can go through all of those comments, because feedback is great. You can get it now. Your cabinet will go through, and they can share with you the things even that are negative, but that are not mean-spirited.

Brene: So the physics of vulnerability, if you're brave enough, often enough you're going to fall. You're going to risk falling, you're going to fall.

Oprah: You're going to fall.

Brene: Right. What has been one of your toughest falls?

Oprah: Oh, boy. I would say starting out with this network was a tough fall. I'd come off the glory and the victory of 25 years of the Oprah Show and was trying to put together the pieces of building a network without the right pieces. I really was trusting other people's ideas about how to do it and it wasn't until I had the good sense to bring in my own team of people who I'd been working with. Whom I've been working with for the past decade that things started to actually fall into place for me. But that was really bitter, talk about not reading comments. I had spent 25 years of you know sometimes get negative publicity and certainly had the tabloids and all of that to deal with. But I had never dealt with what felt like vitriolic nananana look at you. You've fallen, you're not on top anymore. You're not as good as you think you are. All of that stuff that came in the media immediately after I ended the Oprah Show and started the climb to build this network. That was a really, really tough time.

Brene: Shame?

Oprah: I guess the word shame yes would apply. Because part of it was I was thinking, wow, I can't pull it together. I can't figure out what's going to work. So part of the shame and embarrassment was not knowing what I didn't know.

Brene: And coming from a place where.

Oprah: Coming from a place where I knew it.

Brene: You knew it.

Oprah: Like the back of my hand. Doing that show for 25 years. It was as easy as breathing to me. I literally could close my eyes, you can put me on the set, and I could stand there and talk to the yard. It just was as easy as breathing. So yes, I had some serious come to Jesus talks with myself about it. Part of what I understood was happening is I know how the world works, is the world is reflecting you back to you? The negative speaks, the sometimes vitriolic negative speak. I mean, people have panels of discussions sitting up on shows, talking about what had happened. What has happened to the Queen of Talk.

Brene: Yes, the postmortem on the fall.

Oprah: The post-mortem of the fall. I saw one thing in, and I can't even remember the headline now, cause I was so like, I've got to dismiss it. But it was Oprah doesn't own herself anymore or Oprah doesn't and shamed me. That headline devastated me, shamed me, so I said, I'm not going to look at anything else. I'm not going to, because I already know what I'm going through, I already know what it is. It's happening because you also think all those things. Nobody's saying anything to you that you haven't felt too.

Brene: Oh my God! You bought into the narrative.

Oprah: Yes and we're going to turn that narrative around. I had David Zasloff actually said to me when one day, this narrative changes today, we're changing this narrative. It's true. Yes, that was a very difficult, that was a time that required a lot of courage and not just courage to keep going, but courage to okay, what does this really mean? What is this really trying to say to me, **Brene:** You know shame has two tapes, never good enough and who do you think you are? When you're getting ready to do something brave in your life, what is the shame gremlin message that you have to be the most cautious about? The one that you have to say, I'm turning this down.

Oprah: I've lived with, who do you think you are my whole life? Not from myself as much as what was reflected to me. Because what do you think you are? You're a little colored girl from Mississippi. Who do you think you are? You're sitting up on national television. Who do you think you are that you can have it? It's the who do you think you are.

Brene: What is your response to that?

Oprah: My response is I used to fear hearing the term, who do you think you are? Or you must be pretty full of yourself.

Brene: Big for your britches.

Oprah: Too big for your britches. Now I work at being full. I want to be so full I am overflowing. So when you see me coming, it ought to make you proud. To borrow a line from my

Angelou's phenomenal woman, "When you see me coming, it ought to make you proud." What you see is a woman so full, I'm overflowing with enough to share with everybody else. I'm going to own the fullness without ego, without arrogance.

Brene: That's beautiful.

Oprah: But with an amazing sense of gratitude, that I've been born at a time where I am female on the planet, and I have the great pleasure and freedom to fill myself up.

Brene: We're going to take a really sharp right turn. If you could put anything on a t-shirt, what would it be?

Oprah: It would be love is the cure.

Brene: You have a soundtrack for your life. Tell me one song that would absolutely have to be on that soundtrack.

Oprah: Amazing Grace,

Brene: Do you have a favorite version?

Oprah: There is only in my mind one version, Wintley Phipps, sang Amazing Grace on my front lawn. In 2005, when I brought all the legends who had represented what it meant to be excellent in my childhood. There was Maya Angelou.

Brene: Oh God!

Oprah: And Coretta Scott King and there was Dorothy Hyde and there was Roberta Flack. There was Diana Ross and there was Ruby Dee and Cicely Tyson and Wintley Phipps saying Amazing Grace on my front lawn.

Brene: Favorite room in your house?

Oprah: Well, first of all, I love my house.

Brene: I love your house too. I got to say.

Oprah: I got to say, oh my goodness! Favorite room in my house. Oh, God, I love this question. It makes me smile. Favorite room in my house is my bedroom office sitting room. That is where I spend the most time. First of all, there's light coming in and usually I'm working for my desk, literally with my bare feet up on the desk.

Brene: That's good.

Oprah: That's my power position. When I was filming The Color Purple, I had written, I still have the journal, that one day, I really hope I have enough money to have a home with beautiful things, in a beautiful surroundings that matches my beautiful spirit. I wrote it down in the summer of 1985.

Brene: There is the power of intention.

Oprah: There is the power of intention. But having a home, surrounded by beautiful things that matched my beautiful spirit.

Brene: What's the best thing about being your age?

Oprah: Oh gosh. The best thing about being my age is I have reached a point where I live in the space of awareness of the time that I might have remaining. You know you have more time that you have lived, unless there's going to be some big DNA discovery, then you actually have to live. So it makes the time that you have right now, even more precious and there's an awareness. You know, one of the great, great, great things for me doing interviews all these years on the Oprah Show and on OWN, was that I got to learn from other people's mistakes. I paid really close attention to the stories.

Brene: That's powerful.

Oprah: I paid really close attention, and I learned as you know, some people watch a lot of shows. I think probably Gayle watched more shows than anybody cause she would watch every day and exercise. But she not even saw every single day.

I was there every day and I got to hear everything and everybody. All the theories and all the stories all the layers and layers of dysfunction along with people's victories, their triumphs.

Brene: Oh yes the wisdom.

Oprah: Wisdom and I took it in. I was a student of it. I wasn't just a talk show host, I was a student. I became a student of life, other people's lives and how to live well by listening to those stories. I paid real attention and I'm at a point in my life where I can literally rejoice in the knowing space that I hold. There's a sense of confidence that can only come, I think when you know, and are assured that you are living life well. Not from the point of view of having a lot of things, but living life from the center space, when you're living bravely. When you're living bravely because you're living your truth.

Brene: I mean I really believe that we make up stories about other people's fearlessness. But there's not enough conversation about the falls and the hurt and the climb back up and the shame. Your show was one of the places where people had those conversations.

Oprah: Yes, it was during my show that I absolutely learned for sure for myself, through other people's stories, that there really isn't any such thing as failure. I could see the thread of courage that was required every time you fell down. I could also see that failure was just there to inform you to move in a different direction. It's just there to say, hey, not this way, over here. Not over there, wrong place. Once I figured that out, it became easier to be braver.

Brene: You know what I love about you, one of many things. But what I really love about you is if I had to describe you to someone, I would say above all else you're both a teacher and a student.

Oprah: Me too. I wouldn't have thought of that, but that is absolutely the truth.

Brene: You know that and which I think, I really actually believe all good teachers are the best students. Like all good writers are good readers usually. But it's weird almost how you straddle that tension. You have so much to impart, but you are one of the most curious people I've ever met in my life. Thank you for being brave with your life really. You make me braver, and you make the world a braver place.

OPRAH WINFREY

Empowerment Stage ESSENCE Festival
(2016)

Announcer: Well, I'm here to introduce our final guest of the day, I must say she a pretty big deal! Yes, in short she is a media mogul, a talk show host, a network owner, a philanthropist, a producer, an actress, and an inspiration to us all. You know actually she is a legend. Yes, and what I know for sure is that she is definitely worth the wait.

Oprah: Essence! Essence! Hello! My first time here, what took me so long? What took me so long? All I got to say is it's beyond happiness to be here and pretty women wonder where my secret lies. Cause I'm not that cute or built to suit a fashion model's size. But when I start to tell them, they say, girl, you telling lies! I said no, it's in the reach of my arms, it's in the span of my hips. It's in the curl of my lips and when you see me walking it ought to make you proud and you understand why my head's never bowed. It's in the bend of my hand, the need for my care, because I'm a woman, phenomenally phenomenal.

Sometimes I walk into a room just as cool as you please and do a man, the fellas need to stand to fall down on their knees. Then they'd start swarming all around me like a hive of honeybees. I say, whoa, it must be this fine, my eyes. Could be the flash of my teeth, the swing in my waist or just the joy in my feet, because I'm a woman. Phenomenal, phenomenal woman. You are Essence, phenomenal women and a few cool men. Thank you. A few cool men have a seat. I want you to know that I've been planning on coming here for the past six months. Iyanla Vanzant asked me personally to come and join her here on the Empowerment Stage. Back in January, she was at my house, and she said, I want you to do something you've never been. You're always working, make the time come be with me sister, as my special guest.

So I was supposed to be y'all surprise and then Iyanla was speaking in Jamaica and unfortunately started having stomach pains, and continue to speak, even though she wasn't feeling well. By the time she got on the plane to come back to the United States, they had to have ambulances waiting at the airport for her. She had an emergency surgery and she's now doing fine, but could not fly. Could not fly and be here with all of us today. If y'all see my bra showing please let me know, thank you. Donna. Karan. I was going to be the surprise and now I am surprised having to speak to all of you myself. But I feel a sense of joy about it because from the time I landed last night and hit the elevator, it's like the best family reunion you ever had, with all of the relatives you didn't know you had, and a lot of the relatives you really, really, really like. That's what the Essence Festival feels like to me.

So just for a few moments on the Empowerment Stage, I wanted to leave you with hopefully some words of empowerment, because often when I'm introduced, people say things like how many awards I've gotten a lot of them thank you very much. They say how many years I did the Oprah Show and all the accomplishments that go on people's lists. But because this is an empowerment stage, I want to leave you hopefully with something that you can take home that not only empowers, but emboldens you to live the life that God intended. Because this is what people don't know, because you can't tell everybody. I am who I am. One black woman, my hand in God's hand trusting in that word, because that word never failed me. I got to where I am and I stand as I am as Maya Angelou often says in her poem; To our Grandmothers, every time you see me, I come as one, but I stand as 10,000.

It's just not me standing up here. It's my mother, my grandmother, her mother, the mother before her, her grandfather, every uncle who prayed. Every sister who cried, every aunt who sacrifice, those whose names made the history books. Those whose names never could make the history books, who allowed me to come as one and stand as 10,000. Oftentimes, when I walk into a room, just as cool as you please and I can't see another black face in a 50-mile radius, I stand and sit at the boards as one, but I'm bringing the 10,000 behind me. Because I not only know who I am, but I also know whose I am.

Anything you hear about me that feels good, sounds good. You think about, I wonder what Oprah's doing, how's she doing? I am living the dream and I want you to live the dream because I'm not living the dream because I'm special. I'm living the dream because I was obedient to the call of the dream.

I want you to leave here today thinking about what is the dream for you. What is God's dream for you? What does the creator's dream hold for you? Often we spend our lives wishing and hoping and hoping and wishing and desiring things. This is what I know for sure, you don't get what you wish for. You don't even get what you hope for, you get what you believe.

What is it you believe and know to be God's dream for you? I've live in the dream, I'm living in the space of this dream and dream good, dream good. The dream is greater than anything that I could have imagined. You know when I was a little girl, my father on Sunday mornings after church. He was a deacon, so he thought he had to say goodbye to every single person. We were the last car leaving the parking lot, in the green Oldsmobile, and we would drive through the white people's neighborhoods.

I used to dream the dream driving through the white people's neighborhoods. We drive through the white people's neighborhoods, and you'd see their fancy houses, some of them had gates, but all of them had trees. I remember when I first came to Baltimore, I met a friend. Hello, Baltimore in the house! When I first came to Baltimore, I made friends with a wonderful woman named Arlene Wiener. She was the wealthiest person I'd ever met, and I went to her house and parked in the driveway, there was a Corvette and there was a

BMW and there was a Mercedes. I went whoa! Arlene's rich. At Arlene's house, once I got inside, I could see from her kitchen window, six trees in the front yard, and I thought, oh rich people have trees. When I get rich, I'm going to get me some trees. Everybody wants to get cars and pocketbooks and shoes, but I want me some trees.

As life would have it, I was standing in my kitchen window, about three years ago in California, making coffee in the morning. I was looking out the window and saw the six trees. But listen to me, I was making the coffee, I saw the six trees. I went out on the porch to actually count the six trees, and this is what I noticed. That I could dream the six, but beyond the six trees in my kitchen window are 3,687 trees. How do I know? Cause I had them count it. I had them count it cause I say, I want to know how many trees out there. I dreamed the 6, that's as much as my small mind and my imagination could hold for myself. I dreamed the six, but God can see beyond the six. Can see beyond the six, because there was a bigger dream for me.

I'm here to tell you there is a bigger dream for your Essence. There's a bigger dream and so the key, the secret, the magic is to surrender to God's dream for you. To quit fighting against, pushing against, disallowing against, resisting against, and trying to tell the creator, the universal forces, divine intelligence, what you are supposed to do and get still and know for sure what his dream, the dream is for you.

When I was about eight years old, I grew up in the church and I was going to one of those women's day. You know we have church all day long: I've been to Sunday school and then afternoon, they were having a Women's Tea from the Women's Board and they were having tea and the little girl that was supposed to be there to do a recitation had gotten ill. So they said to my stepmother, we need a little girl, can Oprah come back and do a recitation this afternoon? My stepmother said, yes, I'll have her back here this afternoon. Church isn't over till 1:30, so by four o'clock. I had gone home and learned to recite Invictus by William Ernest Henley. Now it starts out, 'out of the night that covers me black as a pit from pole to pole, I thank whatever gods may be for my unconquerable soul.'

I was reciting it and doing the pit from pole to pole. I didn't know what I was saying, but at the end of the poem, there is the standard that says, 'it matters not how strait the gate, how charged with punishment the scroll, I am the master of my fate. I am the captain of my soul.' Now my little eight-year-old brain didn't really fully understand the power and depth of those words, but they sounded good enough for me to write them down and put them on my mirror. Those words, 'I am the master of my fate, I am the captain of my soul,' became a mantra for me. What it said is I am responsible for the choices that I make in my life. I am responsible. I am responsible. Obviously, I grew up and was better able to articulate what those words really mean.

I discovered in physics class, those of you who remember physics, the third law of motion, you remember what that is? The third law of motion in physics says, for every action it's called Newton's Law. It says for every action, there is an equal and opposite reaction.

So what does that mean? That means everything that you are putting out into the world, every action, bam! There is an equal and opposite reaction. It means no matter what you do, the energy of what you do, what you say and most important, the energy of who you are is going out into the world, into your home, into your relationships. That energy is always coming back to you. You are responsible for the energy that you are pulling out into the world because that very energy, bam! is coming right back to you every single time, whether you believe it or not, because it is law. It is law! It is law that what you put out into the world is coming back.

Now in our country and many countries all over the world, they call this the golden rule. They say, do unto others, as you would have them do unto you. The truth is whatever you do is already done. The truth is, so when I learned this, that I am the person who gets to control what comes back to me, based upon what I'm putting out. Ms. Sealy tried to tell y'all in The Color Purple. Ms. Sealy said it best, roll Sealy for me. 'Everything you've done to me, it already done to you.' That's real! That's law, that's not just some words that Alice Walker wrote, that is law. Everything you try to do is already done. When I figured that out, oh, what I'm putting out is what's coming back, let me get real clear about what it is I'm putting out, real clear. I read a book about 1989 called Seat of the Soul, and in that book, Gary Zukav talked about the laws of karma, of the laws of cause and effect, the third law of motion.

In that book, he talked about how intention, your intention is always one with the law. Meaning before you even think about a thing, you have an intention for the thing, and that the intention is going to determine the outcome. That's why the same people can go to the same church service, and somebody walked down the aisle just to be seen to put some money in the church and somebody else who just goes and just has a little bit to offer.

The intention with which you give, the intention with which you serve, determines the outcome. When I figured that out, I went whoa! I changed everything I did on my show. I called in the producers, and I said, from this day forward, I will no longer be speaking to the KKK. I will no longer be speaking to people who are fighting each other in a way that it is damaging to the character of myself and other people who watch. From this day forward, I'm only going to do intentional television.

They're like, how are we going to do that and still win? The reason we remain number one for 25 straight years, is because every single day, I would have a pre-show meeting and have the producers come in and state to me, what is your intention? How do we want to use whoever's on this show, whatever is happening on this show to serve the audience in a way that fulfills the mission of uplifting, enlightening, encouraging as well as entertaining. If it doesn't do that, then I can't do it. I can't put my name on it. I use this principle of intention for everything, I don't do anything without thinking about what is the real reason. What is the real motivation? What is the energy of my intention that's going to go into my thoughts and action, and then be returned back to me. It is law, it's law.

The very first time I practiced this principle, there was a woman on the show whose daughter had been murdered by her boyfriend. I went into the green room, I said, I'm going to see if this works. I said can you tell me what's your intention? I said, tell me what's your intention in being here and she said, what do you mean? I'm here because your producers asked me to come. I said but what is the reason you said yes? What did you intend when you said yes? She said, I wanted people to know, everybody asked me about my daughter's death and how she was murdered by her boyfriend. But I wanted people to know that my daughter was a real person. My daughter was loved, and she loved us. I want people to know that my daughter had a life that goes beyond her death, that's bigger than her death. That her life was bigger than her death.

I said okay, I can help you with that intention, let me tell you what I intend. I intend to literally exploit your daughter's life to tell the story in such a way that every other 16-year-old girl who is being abused by her 18-year-old boyfriend will see themselves in the story of your daughter. They will hear that she had a life, they will hear that everything seemed normal on the outside. But see themselves in her story and be able to be empowered by the life and death of your daughter. Every question that I ask you, is not me trying to be just a voyeur, I'm using and asking the questions explicitly for a reason. For an intention to get people to see themselves, that is the first show I won an Emmy for. I will say that this principle of intention I use in everything. For the last interview that I did with Whitney Houston, we did the, Hey girl, how you doing? Oh my God! Oh my God! Good to see you! So-and-so.

Then I say, turn the cameras off. I say Whitney, tell me what is your intention? Why are you doing this interview? Why did you want to sit with me? What is it you want to happen at the end of these two hours? Tell me what it is you want, because I control the mic and I can make sure that happens. I've used that principle for every area of my life. I don't do anything, and I ask that you consider not doing anything that you don't truly intend. Do not allow yourself to be marginalized and defined by other people's agendas and intentions, because the power of your story lies in your personal intention.

It is my intention to fulfill the dream of the creator. It is my intention to live to the highest calling and be pressed to the mark of the highest calling that I have come to do. When you can ask the creator, ask that which made you, you, what is your dream for me? I guarantee you, instead of you trying to define the dream, what is your dream for me? If you're able to lean into to the dream that the universe and all the forces of light and love and power and grace, by all the names that we call God has for you, nobody can touch you. Nobody can touch you. That is the power of your phenomenon.

Now everybody works hard, and everybody has their own dreams. There was a time where I used to spend a lot of energy wanting things. Of course, it's easy for me to say, oh things don't define you because I got a lot of things. Things are nice, I like them, but this is what I learned. When you can surrender to the dream, you get to live in the space of the higher power. You get to live in the space that you purposely have come to earth to claim for yourself.

Around 1984, I was sitting in bed one morning, a Sunday morning, should have been in church, but I wasn't. I was reading the New York Times review of The Color Purple and I thought, whoa! This sounds like a really great book. I got out of bed in my pajamas, put on my galoshes and went to the store to get the copy of The Color Purple. I read The Color Purple in one afternoon, went back to the bookstore, bought every book of The Color Purple.

I took the books to the office, and I said to everybody, y'all got to read this book. Oh my God! You got to read this book Color Purple. I needed a book club, I didn't have one. I pass out the book to everybody I knew, please read The Color Purple, read The Color Purple. Then I start to hear that somebody is going to do a movie about The Color Purple, but I don't know anybody in the movie business. By this time I was on AM Chicago, I don't know anybody. I start praying to God, God, please help me find a way to get into Color Purple. I say, Jesus,

I don't even have to have a speaking part. Cause I went to the movies, and I saw on the movie credits at the last credit, there's something called best boy. I said Jesus, if you just let me be best girl, that'd be all right by me. I can be best girl. I can carry the script. I can help the people with the water, I can do whatever. I started praying for The Color Purple.

As divine law would have it, Quincy Jones comes to Chicago and he is in Chicago for one half of a day, because somebody has filed a suit against Michael Jackson claiming that Billie Jean was their lover and that's not his song. So Quincy had taken the red-eye to Chicago, he was in his hotel room. He was coming out of the shower and the television in his hotel room is on AM Chicago. There sits little chubby me with my Jerri curl, on AM Chicago. Quincy Jones tells Ruben Cannon the casting agent, I think I found Sophia. So I get a call from Ruben Cannon, who says, I'm calling about a movie it's called Moon Song, would you be interested to come and audition? I say, I have not been praying for Moon Song. No, I had not been praying for Moon Song, I've been praying for The Color Purple. He said, well, I think you should come and audition. I go to audition, you know movie people, they make everything all secret. Steven Spielberg didn't want anybody to know he was doing Color Purple.

On the outside of the script, it says Moon Song, but I know all the words by heart. When I opened the script, I know this is The Color Purple, Jesus! This is The Color Purple, yes! I auditioned for The Color Purple: I can't even believe it, they don't just want me to be the water girl or the best girl. They are asking me do I want a part in the movie? Oh, that I'm thinking prayer works, prayer works. But listen to this, three months passed, three months is a long time. I auditioned in February, March, April, May comes, I haven't heard anything. I call Reuben Cannon, I say, Mr. Cannon, I'm sorry sir I haven't heard anything. I expected to hear something by now and Reuben Cannon, African-American man says to me, you don't call me, I call you and I didn't call you. Do you understand that I have real actresses who have auditioned for this part, real actresses. He tells me who just left his office, and I went well, okay, I'm not getting that part. I hang up the phone and I start crying.

I can't believe that God has played this trick on me. I think this is a trick, so I decided that this is because the fat has finally caught up with me. The fat has finally caught up with me and now I must get rid of the fat in two weeks. I am going to go to a fat farm and I'm going to lose 25 pounds. I'm going to drink a lot of green juice, I'm going to have some cleanses and colonics. I also was trying to make peace with it, I said, God, I don't understand. I thought it was for me. You ever had that talk with God? I thought it was for me. I thought it was for me. God, you let me audition with somebody named Harpo. That's my name backwards, Jesus, that was a sign, wasn't it a sign? Then three months pass and then Reuben Cannon says, real actresses have just left his office. I start to pray on the track, I'm out on the track at the fat farm, and I am running around at the track at the fat farm. It starts to rain, y'all know how that is, but I don't even care because I am praying to God to help me to let it go. Help me let it go because now I've become obsessed with it and it's now controlling my life. I start praying, running around the track. I keep hearing this noise and there's nobody on the track, but me and I'm running around the track. I look around and it is my thighs rubbing together. It's my thighs, my thighs are rubbing together causing this thunderous sound.

There's nobody on the track, so then I really start to cry. Oh Lord, help me! Help me let it go. Help me let it go. Help me let it go. God, help me let it go. You ever did this prayer where you say okay Lord, okay, I'm going to let it go. Then you get up and you go, well I think I still got a little bit of it. Help me let it go, but I'm not going to be able to see the other actress in my part. I won't be able to see it. I won't be able to see Color Purple, just can't never see it the rest of my life. I won't be able to see it. Then I started, I don't know where it came from (singing) I Surrender All. I Surrender All, all to thee my blessed savior, I surrender all. I sang and I cried, and I prayed some more, until I could reach the point where not only will I be able to go to the movie, but I can bless the other actress. I can bless her, I can say I bless you. I bless you. I bless you with this. I surrender all, I surrender all, all to thee my blessed savior, I surrender all.

I tell you in my greatest testimony that the instant I laid that thing down. I'm telling you when I laid it down, when I laid it down and it didn't have me anymore, it had no control over me anymore. I didn't feel anything about it anymore, when I let it go, when I intentionally surrendered it to the power that was greater than I could ever know. The instant that happened, a woman comes running out of the cafeteria screaming Ofree! Is your name Ofree? For 10 years, nobody could pronounce my name. I said yes, she says somebody is on the telephone for you, he says his name is Spielberg. I get to the phone, he says I hear you're at a fat farm. I said no sir, this is a health retreat. He says, I'd like to see you in my office in California tomorrow. This was in Wisconsin I was, I would like to see you in my office and if you lose a pound, you could lose this part. No problem, I have no problem, not losing a pound. Honey, I packed my bags and I stopped at the Dairy Queen. I got three scoops just in case I'd lost a half a pound and the next day I was in Steven Spielberg's office, and he said you're hired.

The Color Purple was a life-changing event for me, because it taught me that you can dream of the dream and that God can have a bigger dream. But most importantly, it taught me the power of surrender. It taught me when you've done everything you can do, you don't just have to stand. When you've prayed and cried, stood and tried some more, sacrificed and wanted and dreamed and held on, believed and got turned down and turned back then turned around. It taught me that when you've done everything you can do, surrender all, surrender all. Cause there's a bigger dream, there's a bigger dream waiting for you, just waiting for you to step into it. Your life is big, your life is huge, and we spend so much time wanting to be in somebody else's life. You don't get honored, you don't get revered, you don't get celebrating, wanting what somebody else has because that which created you, divine intelligence that dreamed you from before your ancestors ever knew they would become your ancestors. That which dreamed the seed of you, wants you to know how special, how wondrous, how mysterious, how complex, how glorious, how phenomenal you are.

You get no credit messing in somebody else's territory or trying to have power over something you have no control. Another one of my favorite teachings is The Wizard of Oz, when the Wicked Witch of the West says, go away from here because you don't have any power here. You have no power in any territory other than your own; oh, but you are the master of that. You get to be the master of your own fate. You get to be the captain of your own soul and if you just manage that, if you just took care of your territory, oh, the glorious, glorious, glorious, wondrous, wondrous opportunities and possibilities that are waiting for you.

The question is, what are you resisting? What are you pushing against? What are you not allowing? What are you blocking because you have this idea of who and what you're supposed to be, instead of leaning into the dream that's already been created and waiting for you. It's waiting for you and the second, I mean it's an instant thing. It's a shift in the way you see yourself and the power from which you have come.

I went through some tough times after I left the Oprah Show. I made a conscious decision that I did not want to be sitting on TV with the Oprah Show and y'all saying she should have left that show. That show was really good two years ago. I made a conscious decision that when I felt I had said all that I could say, and the audience had heard it, that I would move on and that I would not spend my life regretting or trying to hold on to what used to be or hold on to what I had.

I dreamed this dream of starting a network and in the beginning it was a struggle. It was a struggle because honest-to-goodness, I did not know what I was doing. I was trying to figure it out. I thought that the Oprah Show audience would follow us to OWN, then I realized y'all didn't have cable. If you had cable, you did not have the OWN package. So it took me a minute and unlike most people who you get to have your mistakes in private, something don't go right in your life, you get to sulk about it in private. If I make a mistake, it's on the CNN crawl or the CNN news.

When I was in the climb and there were so many wonderful owners, I see Cheryl Action Jackson here. There were so many wonderful owners, people who said, oh, we're going to stand with you, we're going to stand by you. Thank you, Roland Martin. There were so many people who said, listen, we believe that this can happen. I dreamed the dream, along with Tyler Perry, who was my friend who came to me and said, Tyler! Tyler said, I'm going to help you out cause Tyler can go home and write a script and direct it produce it and shoot it and do it for less money than anybody in Hollywood. We started with the foundation of having Have-Nots, If Loving you is Wrong, Love Thy Neighbor, Mama Hattie. Then I started to dream another dream about scripted television, because in the beginning I was told you couldn't do it. Couldn't do it, didn't have enough money to do it. I dreamed a dream, I read Proverbs 11:28 that says, 'Those who trust in their riches will fall, but the righteous will rise and thrive like a green leaf.' Now we have this remarkable series every Wednesday night at 10, Greenleaf.

Lynn Whitfield's in the house. Lynn Whitfield playing Lady Mae, where are you Lynn Whitfield? Sister Lynn Whitfield. When I first read that very first script, I heard Lynn's voice in my head and I said, Lord, please let Lynn be available. If you love me Jesus, let Lynn be available. Jesus loves me. Thank you, Lynn Whitfield. Then this happened, I was sitting on my porch looking out at the trees with Ava DuVernay. Now Ava had just finished doing Selma and I was trying to convince her to come sit on the porch, take a break, just take a week Ava, come up. Just relax a minute, because this is what we do, particularly as women people, I can't speak to men because I've never been one, but as women people we'll run ourselves empty, this I know because I've done it. You want to have your cup overflowing, so you have enough to give to everybody else and you can't keep giving from an empty cup.

I had this conversation with Ava, and she listened to me. Ava, come on up here, Ava. Ava came to my house, and I said just relax, I won't bother you. Cause you can sit on the porch, and I got my own porch, and you can sit over there. I presented her with his idea, I was reading this book called, Queen Sugar by Natalie Baszile. I then went to Ava and said Ava, I think, I think this one actually makes a really good series. At first she was like, ah, I don't know, let me see. Then she said, yes I think I could do something with it. Ava DuVernay everybody, Ava DuVernay! Thank you. Let me ask you this, I haven't asked this of you actually really. What was your intention when you said yes?

Ava DuVernay: My intention was to, it was really about OWN. I didn't like that people thought that it wasn't as valuable and as beautiful as I saw it. I thought if there was anything I could give to it and give to this woman who had given so much to me, I can make a television show for this network that I saw as beautiful to help contribute to everyone else seeing its beauty. What it ended up giving me was just so much I can cry just thinking about it. The experience of making Queen Sugar really became a gift for me, not even a gift to her. I thank you for it. Yes, I do.

Oprah: There's a wonderful quote from Nina Shaw who happens to be isn't she your?

Ava DuVernay: She's my attorney yes.

Oprah: Your attorney. There's a wonderful quote that Nina Shaw actually said at the Essence Luncheon that I now use all the time. She says; if you want to be an empowered woman, empower other women.

Ava DuVernay: Yes.

Oprah: That is what we have done on this project with Queen Sugar, because not only did Ava DuVernay create it and direct the first two episodes and manage everything in production, along with a whole team, but she empowered and hired all female directors for Our Queen Sugar.

Ava DuVernay: That's Queen Sugar. I like to bring up the cast of Queen Sugar.

Oprah: The cast of Queen Sugar come on up. I just want to say the fact that this series and Greenleaf. Lynn come on up here too cause we can't see you. Lynn, you still there? Lynn, join us up here cause we couldn't see you. Fact that Lady Maye Greenleaf and Queen Sugar is happening and happening on a network that carries my name, it's God at his finest working with me and working for me. I just want to thank all of you who've supported me all these years. Supported the network, supported us who believe in the dream of what we as a people can do.

Thank you so much. Thank you, Essence!

OPRAH WINFREY

Agnes Scott Colleges 128th Commencement
(2017)

Wow! Thank you. Thanks President Kiss. Morning Agnes Scott! I got to give it to you all. You all do it. You all do it right, I got to say this. You get up, you get out. You get it on, you get it over and out into the world. By noon today, you'll be launched into the world. Congratulations, class of 2017!

I'm really happy to be here. As President Kiss said, this isn't my first visit. I was here in the summer filming for the Immortal Life of Henrietta Lacks over, I think it was it Rebecca Hall. It was 104 degrees, we were pretending it was winter. So when I woke up and saw the clouds this morning, I was like thank you, Lord! I want to say a special thank you to the Board of Trustees. Every one of you whom I met today and said thank you to me, well thank you to you. Thank you, board of trustees. Especially to you, Beth Daniel Holder, thank you so much as the chairman. Thank you, faculty. I love what you do.

All my life before I became interested in television, I thought I was going to be a teacher or a professor. I think it is the most noble profession there is. I think to do what you do changes the world on a daily basis, so I thank you. All of you gorgeous women of Agnes Scott, thank you for having me, but the truth is I was coming anyway. Whether you had invited me here to speak or not I was coming. This was my year to come because as, President Kiss has said, one of my daughter girls, I call them all daughter girls. Because when I was calling them my daughters on social media, people were like, Oprah, you didn't raise daughters. You didn't have no daughters. They're not your daughters. They are my daughter girls.

They're my daughter girls and I didn't raise them from birth. God knew that that wouldn't work out for me, but I got them at the perfect age when they were like 12, all potty trained and stuff. My daughter girl has had the great privilege of growing and blossoming here at Agnes Scott, and I want you to know that at my school, the Oprah Winfrey Leadership Academy for Girls, every year we're graduating another class of girls. I now have 179 girls in college, 20 of them came to the United States. Ten are graduating this year. I have five graduations next week in four different states. So Agnes Scott, you got me fresh. This is the fresh version, see how I'm holding up around June 18th after the ninth one.

One of the 10 called me recently all tentative like, oh Mamo. I'm so sorry, I'm so stressed. I wasn't able to complete one of my courses, so I'm not going to graduate. I went, yes! You are stressed and you can't graduate in June? I only have nine graduations. Fantastic. I sent her three dancing emojis. Let me say when I say I'm happy to be here, I really am. I'm thrilled to be here. Not like most people, they get up and say. "I'm so very happy to be here." "Distinguished guests, I'm so happy to be here." I'm really thrilled because one of my girls who's graduating next week sent me this message saying, Mom Oprah. We've been through a lot. Thank you for believing in me and seeing what others couldn't and when I walk across that stage, this is for us. We did this.

I would like to say that goes for every parent in this room, every guardian, every trusted loved one here today, this is for you. Those of you who are here and those who are past even, thank you for encouraging and supporting and being there for our daughters. For being often a balm in Gilead for them. For these daughters who've grown into these incredible young women that you barely recognize when they come home, right before our eyes. Because let me just tell you this, my daughter girl came here and when she came her name was Pretty. I knew her as Pretty, I found her in a township in South Africa and she was known as Pretty.

When I was meeting here in the President's office, this is after they had sent me every possible Scotty piece of merchandise. I had Scotty hats and scarves and gloves and Scotty towels. I had a Scottie microwave, I mean there's just lots of Scotty merchandise. I was stopping in to say thank you, you can stop now. I was sitting in president Kiss's office, and she was telling me about Satoko. Satoko, who's such an inspiring student and Satoko has gone overseas. I'm thinking, who the hell is she talking about? She must have me confused with someone else. It turns out Satoko is Satoko Mele who used to be Pretty when she came to the school. That's what happens when you come to Agnes Scott. A girl who was just happy to be called Pretty.

She gets educated here and thinks more deeply about what really matters to herself. She learns to live more honorably, engage in the intellectual and social challenges of our times. She comes through this process and wants to own herself in the fullness of her name. She wants to lay claim to her calling and have the fullness of her name spoken out loud even if you can't pronounce, Satoko Mele. That's what happens when you come here to Agnes Scott, you leave as a more deepened human with higher standards, striving to realize your social and your academic responsibility to the community and our world. Whoa! Does the world need you right now? Really the struggle is real out there, it's real.

The struggle to remain compassionate and the struggle to remain committed and the struggle to be constructively engaged. That's the challenge that you're in for class of 2017, but I'm betting on you. Agnes Scott women, I'm betting on you. Particularly this class of 2017, I'm betting that you will break new ground to move us all forward and we need your passion, we do. We need your passion to serve, and I was so thrilled to hear that so many of you have signed up for the Peace Corps. Many of you have signed up for Teach for America, all of these service oriented opportunities. But I say this to you. I'm here to tell you that you don't have to necessarily join the Peace Corps or Teach for America or go work for an NGO in a Third World country, to live a life that's full of service. You don't have to do that.

OPRAH WINFREY

I was not your age, but about 30 years old, I started to realize that it was my whole life. Not just parts of my life, just not parts of what I was doing, but my whole life was a prayer. My whole life is an offering in service, first to yourself to become a fully actualized human being. You do that through your actions and your interactions with others. But when I started to realize it's not just what I do, but it's how I do it. It's how I'm not just praying on my knees, but I live in a state of humility on my knees, in service to the higher calling of my life, that things started to change. You know so many people are worried about building a brand. I hear kids on social media talking about their brand, and I used to really resent the word when people would say to me, oh, you have this brand because I never even thought about a brand. I just thought about day in and day out making the best, right choice for me.

But now I embrace it, because I recognize people see me as a brand. But for me, it's not a business, it is a question of what do you stand for. I will say this, you're nothing if you're not the truth. I've made a living. I've made a life. I made a fortune really, it's fantastic! All good, from being true to myself. If I could leave you with any message today, that is it. The biggest reward is not financial benefits, though it's really good, you can get a lot of great shoes. Nothing wrong with great shoes. Those of you who have a lot of shoes know that having great shoes and a closet full of shoes or cars or houses or square footage, doesn't fill up your life. It doesn't but living a life of substance can. Substance through your service, your offering of your whole self. The baseline for how you live a life of substance is whatever is the truth for you. What do you stand for?

When I was saying to my girls last night, some of them had come in to support Satoko Mele, what should I talk to you about? They were like any one of the things you've told us over a hundred times will work. I usually go to my school in South Africa once a year, and I teach a class called Life 101, where for a week I just talk about what I think you need to know to go out in the world. I'm trying to distill it for you today and I would say that having compassion for other people is at the top of that list. I would say commitment is at the top of that list and also a spirit of constructive engagement. By compassion, I don't just mean sympathy, it certainly isn't pity. It's being present and it's also feeling with other beings.

You know during the years of the Oprah Show, I interviewed over 37,000 people one-on-one. So, whenever I'm telling my girls anything and they say, oh, they start rolling their eyes. I go, "I'm the only person you're going to talk that has talked to 37,000 people. So, if I were you, I would pay attention." But during all those years of talking to over 37,000 people one on one, I could feel what they were feeling so strongly, sometimes it made me sick, literally. I had to learn how to feel how others were feeling, feel with others, which is what it means to be compassionate. To feel with others, without taking in all of their stuff. Being compassionate means, I feel with you. It is one of the greatest qualities in the world to have, if you're going to be majoring in what it takes to be a great human being.

I feel with you, means I not only am willing to walk in your shoes, it means my heart beats with yours. It means I see myself in you. It means I may not have shared that circumstance, but I know what heartbreak feels like. I know what pain feels like and all pain is the same. It means I can feel your will to want to do better and be better. I feel and I am with you. In spite of everything that's happened to you, I feel your need to rise. I want to help you rise. I want to rise with you, so compassion is one of them. Commitment is another. You know one of my favorite quotes is Dr. King who says, "Not everybody could be famous, but everybody can be great because greatness is determined by service." I am committed to service, service through my work, service through my life's purpose.

If you make a commitment, a conscious intention to be committed to the work that you do, to the relationships that you have, your life will unfold with such beauty and grace through that commitment. Every day until the very final shows of the Oprah Winfrey Show, I would have the producers come in and tell me ahead of time, what their intention for every show was. Because I figured out around the second year of doing that show, that it wasn't just about being on television and performing. That here was this opportunity, this offering I could give to people, through the service of a television show, to better see themselves through the stories that we're telling and through those stories help themselves to improve their lives.

I started using television as a tool of service. So, as you're trying to figure out what do I do? How should I do it? First of all, I will say this, that when you don't know what to do, my girls have heard this over a hundred times. When you don't know what to do, you do nothing. You get still until you do know. Because if you have to ask everybody else, should I do this? That's whether it's buying a pair of shoes or going with a guy, buying a house, taking a job, should I? When you have to ask everybody else, it means you don't really know the answer fully yourself. You get still, be still and know the answer will come. More than ever, I would have to say I miss the Oprah Winfrey Show. I chose to let it go. I felt that I'd said everything I needed to say after 25 years, and I wanted it to be my decision when I let it go.

But I will say this past year, and now more than ever, I miss it. Because I miss the opportunity for the spirit of constructive engagement that platform offered. Two weeks after the election last year, I went to a dinner in Queens for Oprah Magazine, with a group of women. Half of them were Trump supporters, half of them were Hillary supporters. Nobody wanted to come to breakfast. I was like, it's going to be some great croissants, we're going to have some nice jams ladies. Nobody wanted to sit down and have the croissants. Everybody came in the room all tight and hardened and they were like, well, I've never been this close to these Hilary elitists. I've never been this close. Other people were saying, well, I never sat this close to Trump supporters before, but we're going to do it.

I will tell you, after two and a half hours, I had those women not only eating croissants, sitting around the table, listening to each other's stories. Hearing both sides and by the end, they were holding hands, exchanging, emails and phone numbers and sing and reach out and touch, we're all pretending to be Diana Ross. Which means it's possible, it can happen. I want you to work in your own way to change the world in respectful conversations with others. At a rate and a rhythm that's in tune with the source from which you have come, your truth. I want you to enter every situation aware of its contexts, open to hear the truth of others and most important open to letting the process of changing the world, change you. That is the spirit of constructive engagement.

That's the goal, to be a compassionate woman of substance, to be committed. To have constructive engagement, to live this life of substance. Substance. What I know for sure is if you focus on the substance, the success will come and most importantly, let failure be your friend. There are going to be times of course, where you're going to win a lot. A lot of things are going to go your way, and it's wonderful to bask in that adulation and to feel proud of your successes. But there are also going to be times, the satisfaction that those moments bring nothing can compare to that. Those victories will feed you for years to come and help you stay committed when your tank is sometimes empty. Winning is great. It's fantastic! I love it! I love being number one. I love winning! But it's the times when things go wrong, when you fall or fail that you're actually going to learn the most about yourself.

All those years on the Oprah Show, 25 years, we were the number one show for 25 years and that's because I lived with the intention to serve the audience. The audience came first, every show I would sit with the producers and say, well I can't do that because I can't find the truth of myself in that show. I have to have a thread of truth to be able to hold on to. So, I knew so well the audience, I felt like I was the audience, the audience was me and I felt so connected. Then I ended that, started a new network and failed for a while, and I was really upset with myself. But I will tell you that when I was able to shift the paradigm to start looking at wow! What I have instead of what I don't have. What I have, instead of what I thought I've lost, I was able to begin to turn things around.

But it's those moments of being of uncertainty, it's the moments where all of my mistakes show up on the evening news. You can make a mistake. I can tell if I've done something wrong, it's on the CNN crawl. I can read about it. But learning from the moments where things weren't going so great. Being able to get still to connect with that, which I know is God, the force, the power greater than myself, and to come back and realize that in order to move forward. You move forward by taking the next right step. You don't have to know everything to do, you don't have to know all the steps to make, just what is the next right move. Then there's this, I leave you with this, nobody makes it alone, nobody. I don't care what they look like, I don't care what their Insta posts say. Nobody makes it alone.

You will get nowhere without a spiritual practice. You need a spiritual practice and by that, I mean not necessarily religion. For some people, it is church. For some people, it is meditating, for some people it's dancing, for some people it's singing. But you have got to find a way to nurture that which is the essence of you. You've got to find a way to continually give back to yourself, so that you are a full woman. You want to be a woman who's full of herself. I used to fear that. You know, when I first started out, people would say, oh, she thinks she's just so full of herself. She's so full of herself and I now say, yes, I am. So full, my cup is running over! That's what you want, you want your cup to be so full, it's running over so you have enough to offer others. If you do not have something, a spiritual practice, maybe it's music or dancing or just time for yourself to feed, nurture your own spirit, you'll run out. Your tank will become empty. You will burn out and not have anything left to give.

Set aside space every day to make space for that aspect of your being, which no other single activity you engage in, can fully express. That's all I mean, by spiritual practice, nurture that thing that is the essence of you. I leave you with the words of my mentor teacher, Maya Angelou. I'm thinking of her a lot because it's Mother's Day tomorrow, I'm going to have her on Super Soul, Sunday, for those of you who watch, I learned so much from her. When I finished my school, I was so proud of myself for building this school in South Africa, I went to Maya, and I said, "Maya, that's going to be my greatest legacy, the school." And Maya said, "You have no idea what your legacy will be." I go, I know that, but I really do think that the school is going to be my greatest legacy. And she goes, "You have no idea." So I go, yes, ma'am.

She said this, and I leave this with everybody in the room, graduates, friends of graduates, family. She said your legacy is every life you've touched. Your legacy is every life you've touched. It's not just the big school with your name on it. It's not the awards that you received. It's not the acclaim, it's every single human being you've ever come in contact with. You have left your heart print and your legacy. I remember the story of a man who was a police officer, his heart had stopped, and they weren't even able to get him to the emergency room. They just cut him open on the floor of the hospital, as he was entering the hospital and massage his heart for nine minutes, trying to bring him back. Sounds incredible and unbelievable, but the story he told of having a near-death experience, whether you believe it or not. The impression it left with me was that something happened there.

I don't remember his name, but the story has lingered in my spirit and abides with me. He said, "I didn't see Jesus, but I did have what I thought was my own life review. I was able to feel in a way I cannot explain," he says, "it felt like real time, but I know it couldn't have been, because I wasn't gone for that long. But I was able to feel in what felt like to me, real time, every single thing I ever did. I was able to feel the feelings that I created in other people." "I was a wife beater," he said. "I used to beat my wife and I could not only feel the physical pain I caused her. I felt what I did to her spirit. I broke her heart. So, when I came back and realized I wasn't dead, I decided I'm going to feel things differently. I'm going to try to feel everything with love. I'm going to feel everything with love, so that I can live everything with love." So that's my wish for you, feel everything with love, because every moment you are building your legacy.

OPRAH WINFREY

USC Annenberg Class of 2018

Thank you Wallis Annenberg and a special thank you to Dean Willow Bay for inviting me here today. And to the parents, again I say, and to the faculty, friends, graduates, good morning.
I want to give a special shout out because I was happy that Dean Bay invited me but I was going to be here anyway because one of my lovely daughter girls attends the Annenberg School of Journalism and is getting her masters today, so I was coming whether I was speaking or not. So a special shoutout to a young woman who I met when she was in the seventh grade and it was the first year that I was looking for smart, bright, giving, resilient, kind, open-hearted girls who had "it"—that factor that means you keep going no matter what. And this was the year that I chose everybody individually. And I remember her walking into the office in a little township where we were doing interviews all over South Africa and she came in and recited a poem about her teacher and when she walked out the door I go, "That's an 'it' girl." Thando Dlomo, I'm here to say I am so proud of you. Long way from the township in South Africa and her Aunt has flown 30 hours to be here for this celebration today. Thank you so much.
Today I come bearing some good news and some bad news for anybody who intends to build their life around your ability to communicate. So, I want to get the bad news out first so you can be clear. I always like to get the bad stuff upfront, so

OPRAH WINFREY

here it is: Everything around us, including—and in particular the internet and social media—is now being used to erode trust in our institutions, interfere in our elections, and wreak havoc on our infrastructure. It hands advertisers a map to our deepest desires, it enables misinformation to run rampant, attention spans to run short and false stories from phony sites to run circles around major news outlets. We have literally walked into traffic while staring at our phones.

Now the good news: Many of your parents are probably taking you somewhere really special for dinner tonight. I heard. I can do a little better than that. Now that I have presented some of the bad news, the good news is that there really is a solution. And the solution is each and every one of you. Because you will become the new editorial gatekeepers, an ambitious army of truth seekers who will arm yourselves with the intelligence, with the insight and the facts necessary to strike down deceit. You're in a position to keep all of those who now disparage real news, you all are the ones that are going to keep those people in check. Why? Because you can push back and you can answer false narratives with real information and you can set the record straight. And you also have the ability and the power to give voice, as Dean Bay was saying, to people who desperately now need to tell their stories and have their stories told.

And this is what I do know for sure because I've been doing it a long time: If you can just capture the humanity of the people of the stories you're telling, you then get that much closer to your own humanity. And you can confront your bias and you can build your credibility and hone your instincts and compound your compassion. You can use your gifts, that's what you're really here to do, to illuminate the darkness in our world.

So this is what I also know: This moment in time, this is your time to rise. It is. Even though you can't go anywhere, you can't stand in line at Starbucks, you can't go to a party, you can't go any place where anywhere you turn people are talking about how bad things are, how terrible it is. And this is what I know: The problem is everybody is meeting hysteria with more hysteria and then we're all becoming hysterical and it's getting worse. What I've learned all these years is that we're not supposed to match it or even get locked into resisting or pushing against it. We're supposed to see this moment in time for what it is. We're supposed to see through it and then transcend it. That is how you overcome hysteria. And that is how you overcome the sniping at one another, the trolling, the mean-spirited partisanship on both sides of the aisle, the divisiveness, the injustices, and the out-and-out hatred. You use it. Use this moment to encourage you, to embolden you, and to literally push you into the rising of your life. And to borrow a phrase from my beloved mentor Maya Angelou: Just like moons and like suns, with the certainty of tides, just like hopes springing high, you will rise.

So your job now, let me tell you, is to take everything you've learned here and use what you learned to challenge the left, to challenge the right, and the center. When you see something, you say something, and you say it with the facts and the reporting to back it up. Here's what you have to do: You make the choice everyday, every single day, to exemplify honesty because the truth, let me tell you something about the truth, the truth exonerates and it convicts. It disinfects and it galvanizes. The truth has always been and will always be our shield against corruption, our shield against greed and despair. The truth is our saving grace. And not only are you here, USC Annenberg, to tell it, to write it, to proclaim it, to speak it, but to be it. Be the truth. Be the truth.

So I want to get down to the real reason we're here today. In about an hour and a half, you're going to be catapulted into a world that appears to have gone off its rocker. And I can tell you I've hosted the Oprah show for 25 years, number one show. Never missed a day. Never missed a day. Twenty five years, 4,561 shows. So I know how to talk, I can tell you that, but I was a little intimidated coming here because graduations, it's tough, it's hard trying to come up with something to share with you that you haven't already heard. Any information or guidance I can offer is nothing that your parents or your deans or professors or Siri haven't already provided. So I'm here to really tell you: I don't have any new lessons. I don't have any new lessons. But I often think that it's not the new lessons so much as it is really learning the old ones again and again.

So here are variations on a few grand themes beginning with this: Pick a problem, any problem, the list is long. Here are just a few that are at the top of my list. There's gun violence and there's climate change, there's systemic racism, economic inequality, media bias. The homeless need opportunity, the addicted need treatment, the Dreamers need protection, the prison system needs reforming, the LGBTQ community needs acceptance, the social safety net needs saving, and the misogyny needs to stop. Needs to stop. But you can't fix everything and you can't save every soul. But what can you do? Here and now I believe you have to declare war on one of our most dangerous enemies, and that is cynicism. Because when that little creature sinks its hooks into you, it'll cloud your clarity, it'll compromise your integrity, it'll lower your standards, it'll choke your empathy. And sooner or later, cynicism shatters your faith. When you hear yourself saying, "Ah, it doesn't matter what one person says, oh well, so what, it doesn't matter what I do, who cares?" When you hear yourself saying that, know that you're on a collision course for our culture. And I understand how it's so easy to become disillusioned, so tempting to allow apathy to set in, because anxiety is being broadcast on 157 channels, 24 hours a day, all night long. And everyone I know is feeling it. But these times, these times, are here to let us know that we need to take a stand for our right to have hope and we need to take a stand with every ounce of wit and courage we can muster.

The question is: What are you willing to stand for? That question is going to follow you throughout your life. And here's how you answer it. You put your honor where your mouth is. Put your honor where your mouth is. When you give your word, keep it. Show up. Do the work. Get your hands dirty. And then you'll begin to draw strength from the understanding that history is still being written. You're writing it every day. The wheels still in spin. And what you do or what you don't do will be a part of it. You build a legacy not from one thing but from everything. I remember when I just opened my school in 2007, I came back and I had the great joy of sitting at Maya Angelou's table. She hadn't been able to attend the opening in South Africa. And I said to her, "Oh Maya, the Oprah Winfrey Leadership Academy, that's going to be my greatest legacy." I remember she was standing at the counter making biscuits, and she turned, she put the dough down, and she looked at me and she said, "You have no idea what your legacy will be." I said, "Excuse me? I just opened this school and these girls, and it's going to be… " And she said, "You have no idea what your legacy will be, because your legacy is every life you touch. Every life you touch." That changed me.

And it's true, you can't personally stop anybody from walking into a school with an assault rifle, nor can you singlehandedly ensure that the rights that your mothers and grandmothers fought so hard for will be preserved for the daughters you may someday have. And it'll take more than you alone to pull more than 40 million Americans out of poverty, but who will you be if you don't care enough to try? And what mountains could we move, I think, what gridlock could we eradicate if we were to join forces and work together in service of something greater than ourselves? You know my deepest satisfactions and my biggest rewards have come from exactly that.

Pick a problem, any problem, and do something about it. Because to somebody who's hurting, something is everything. So, I hesitate to say this, because the rumors from my last big speech have finally died down, but here it is. Vote. Vote. Vote. Pay attention to what the people who claim to represent you are doing and saying in your name and on your behalf. They represent you and if they've not done right by you or if their policies are at odds with your core beliefs, then you have a responsibility to send them packing. If they go low, thank you Michelle Obama, if they go low, we go to the polls. People died for that right, they died for that right. I think about it every time I vote. So don't let their sacrifices be in vain.

A couple other thoughts before I go. Eat a good breakfast. It really pays off. Pay your bills on time. Recycle. Make your bed. Aim high. Say thank you to people and actually really mean it. Ask for help when you need it, and put your phone away at the dinner table. Just sit on it, really. And know that what you tweet and post and Instagram today might be asked about at a job interview tomorrow, or 20 years from tomorrow. Be nice to little kids, be nice to your elders, be nice to animals, and know that it's better to be interested than interesting. Invest in a quality mattress. I'm telling you, your back will thank you later. And don't cheap out on your shoes. And if you're fighting with somebody you really love, for God's sakes find your way back to them because life is short, even on our longest days. And another thing, another thing you already definitely know that definitely bears repeating, don't ever confuse what is legal with what is moral because they are entirely different animals. You see, in a court of law, there are loopholes and technicalities and bargains to be struck, but in life, you're either principled or you're not. So do the right thing, especially when nobody's looking. And while I'm at it, do not equate money and fame with accomplishment and character, because I can assure you based on the thousands of people I've interviewed, one does not automatically follow the other.

Something else, something else. You need to know this. Your job is not always going to fulfill you. There will be some days that you just might be bored. Other days, you may not feel like going to work at all. Go anyway, and remember that your job is not who you are, it's just what you are doing on the way to who you will become. Every remedial chore, every boss who takes credit for your ideas -- that is going to happen -- look for the lessons, because the lessons are always there. And the number one lesson I could offer you where your work is concerned is this: Become so skilled, so vigilant, so flat-out fantastic at what you do that your talent cannot be dismissed. And finally, this: This will save you. Stop comparing yourself to other people. You're only on this planet to be you, not someone else's imitation of you. I had to learn that the hard way, on the air, live, anchoring the news. One night in my twenties, when I first started broadcasting, I was 19, moved to an anchor by the time I was 20. I was just pretending to be Barbara Walters. I was trying to talk like Barbara, act like Barbara, hold my legs like Barbara. And I was on the air, I hadn't read the copy fully, and I called Canada, Canahdah. I cracked myself up, because I thought, Barbara would never call Canada Canahdah. And that little breakthrough, that little crack, that little moment that I stopped pretending allowed the real me to come through. Your life journey is about learning to become more of who you are and fulfilling the highest, truest expression of yourself as a human being. That's why you're here. You will do that through your work and your art, through your relationships and love.

And to quote Albert Einstein, "Education is what remains after we forget what we're taught." You've learned a lot here at USC. And when all that you've been taught begins to fade into the fabric of your life, I hope that what remains is your ability to analyze, to make distinctions, to be creative, and to wander down that road less traveled whenever you have the opportunity. And I hope that when you go, you go all in, and that your education helps you to walk that road with an open, discerning mind. Discernment is what we're missing. And a kind heart. You know, there are 7 billion people on the planet right now. And here you are. Your degree from the USC Annenberg School for Communication and Journalism: This degree you're about to get is a privilege. It's a privilege. And that privilege obligates you to use what you've learned to lend a hand to somebody who doesn't get to be here. Somebody who's never had a ceremony like the one you're having this morning.

So I hold you in the light, and I wish you curiosity and confidence. And I wish you ethics and enlightenment. I wish you guts. Every great decision I've ever made I trusted my gut. And goodness.

I wish you purpose and the passion that goes along with that purpose. And here's what I really hope: I hope that every one of you contributes to the conversation of our culture and our time. And to some genuine communication, which means, you have to connect to people exactly where they are; not where you are, but where they are. And I hope you shake things up. And when the time comes to bet on yourself, I hope you double down. Bet on yourself. I hope you always know how happy and how incredibly relieved everybody is in this room is that you've made it to this place, at this time, on this gorgeous day.

Congratulations USC Annenberg Class of 2018!

OPRAH WINFREY

Spellman Commencement Speech
(2018)

The three things that I want to leave with you, just these three, I could do 10, I could do a whole life class, but just these three things will carry you if you let them, first and foremost, knowing who you are, knowing who you are, being able to answer this question, who am I and what do I want?

Who am I really? My answer is I am God's child. I am that which is born of all that is, I am, as Peter Chardin said, a spiritual being, having a human experience come trailing the breath of the ancestors yet, but trailing the breath of the angels and understanding that because I am connected to the source of all that is. All that is possible is possible for me.

That's who I am and what do I want? I don't want to just be successful in the world. I don't want to just make a mark or have a legacy. The answer to that question for me is I want to fulfill the highest, truest expression of myself as a human being. I want to fulfill the promise that the creator dreamed when he dreamed the cells that made up me. What do I want? You must have some kind of vision for your life. Even if you don't know the plan, you have to have a direction in which you choose to go. What I've learned is that it's a great metaphor for life. You want to be in the driver's seat of your own life because if you're not, life will drive you. So knowing who you really are. In this space and time that we embody, that's number one. What do you want? Who are you?

Number two. You must find a way to serve. Martin Luther King said that not everybody can be famous, but everybody can be great, because greatness is determined by service. Now, we live in a world where everybody wants to be famous and where we admire people for just being famous. We think being known brings us value. The truth is, all of that will fade in time. In three years, you won't be able to name the housewives of Atlanta. The real truth is that service is significance.

Service and the significance that you bring to your service is that which is lasting, so to be able to whatever your occupation or job or talent or gift is, our honorees today getting doctor degrees to apparently opposite fields, HIV and AIDS and the spoken word. But what they have in common is service, using the spoken word in service to the community and the world, using your knowledge and information about HIV and AIDS and medicine in service to the world.

And if you look at all the most successful people in the world, whether they know it or not, they have that paradigm of service. Everybody's talking about Mark Zuckerberg and IPO. Service, Jay-Z, rapid service through the word to people through song for many years.

I was really just happy to be on TV and people would stop and say, oh, you on TV again? I'm on TV. I like being on TV. It's a nice job. And it was about the time that I received my honorary doctorate from Spelman around 1993. So I don't know if that had something to do with it. I thought of myself as Dr. Winfrey. I went back and I took a long look at what it was I was doing on TV and made a decision that I was no longer going to just be on TV, but I was going to use TV as a platform, as a force for good and not be used by TV.

And I will tell you my decision. To make that significant change in the way I operated on television, using television as a service changed my career exponentially. Service through medicines, service through art, using whatever it is you produce your product as a way of giving back to the world when you shift the paradigm of whatever it is you choose to do to service and you bring significance to that success, will, I promise you value service and significance equal success. That's number two.

Number three, it's so simple but so hard to do. Always do the right thing. Be excellent people. Notice, think of how you notice. You go to Taco Bell, somebody gives you extra napkins and some sauce. You notice you want to go back to that person because even at Taco Bell, excellence shows itself, be excellent. Let excellence be your brand. Everybody talks about building a brand. I never even knew what that was. When people say you're a brand, I would say, no, I'm just Oprah.

What I recognize now is that my choice to in every way, in every example, in every experience, is to do the right thing. The excellent thing is what has created the brand. What I know is that when you are excellent, you become unforgettable people remember you, you stand out regardless of what it is, you become an unforgettable woman.

That is what we all want. We want to be unforgettable and not forgettable. So doing the right thing even when nobody knows you're doing the right thing, will always be the right thing to you, I promise you that. Why? Because the third law of motion is always at work for every action, there's an equal and opposite reaction that is so true in all of our lives. You just have to do the right thing and the right thing will follow you even when people don't support it.

I remember many times on my show, there are many shows you never saw, and the reason you didn't see them is because I got the last vote. I remember in 2010, my team, hardest-working team in television, had done this interview with a woman who turns out she was a Sunday school teacher by day and a sex addict at night. They were like, you won't believe it. We got her going out and we got her with the men. We get to show her and she was willing to show us everything. I sat down with a woman for an interview that was taped and during the process of the interview, I said, why are you doing this? She said, oh, I want to help people. I want to tell my story and I want to help people. I said, do you have children? She says, yes, I have a 10 year old son. I knew right then this is never going to see the light of day. So we got off the air and I said to the lady, we are not going to air that show.

She said, why? My producer said why? She knew she was being filmed. She knew what she was saying, she knows. I said because her son will never get over it. It's not worth a rating point to me. Not worth the rating point to me to know that there's a 10 year old boy who's destroyed because his mother went on The Oprah Winfrey Show and told all her business.

You do the right thing even when other people think it may not be. And oftentimes when you make a decision to do the right thing immediately, you're faced with doubt. Is that the right thing? Was that the right decision? I know was that the right thing? You always know it's the right thing when in the end there is peace, you are rewarded by peace and knowing that you did the right thing.

OPRAH WINFREY

Award for Lifetime Achievement at the Golden Globes
(2018)

In 1964, I was a little girl sitting on the linoleum floor of my mother's house in Milwaukee watching Anne Bancroft present the Oscar for best actor at the 36th Academy Awards. She opened the envelope and said five words that literally made history: "The winner is Sidney Poitier." Up to the stage came the most elegant man I had ever seen. I remember his tie was white, and, of course, his skin was black, and I had never seen a black man being celebrated like that. I tried many, many times to explain what a moment like that means to a little girl, a kid watching from the cheap seats as my mom came through the door bone tired from cleaning other people's houses. But all I can do is quote and say that the explanation in Sidney's performance in "Lilies of the Field":

"Amen, amen."

In 1982, Sidney received the Cecil B. DeMille award right here at the Golden Globes and it is not lost on me that at this moment, there are some little girls watching as I become the first black woman to be given this same award. It is an honor -- it is an honor and it is a privilege to share the evening with all of them and also with the incredible men and women who have inspired me, who challenged me, who sustained me and made my journey to this stage possible. Dennis Swanson who took a chance on me for "A.M. Chicago." Quincy Jones who saw me on that show and said to Steven Spielberg, "Yes, she is Sophia in 'The Color Purple.'" Gayle who has been the definition of what a friend is, and Stedman who has been my rock -- just a few to name.

I want to thank the Hollywood Foreign Press Association because we all know the press is under siege these days. We also know it's the insatiable dedication to uncovering the absolute truth that keeps us from turning a blind eye to corruption and to injustice. To -- to tyrants and victims, and secrets and lies. I want to say that I value the press more than ever before as we try to navigate these complicated times, which brings me to this: what I know for sure is that speaking your truth is the most powerful tool we all have. And I'm especially proud and inspired by all the women who have felt strong enough and empowered enough to speak up and share their personal stories. Each of us in this room is celebrated because of the stories that we tell, and this year we became the story.

But it's not just a story affecting the entertainment industry. It's one that transcends any culture, geography, race, religion, politics, or workplace. So I want tonight to express gratitude to all the women who have endured years of abuse and assault because they, like my mother, had children to feed and bills to pay and dreams to pursue. They're the women whose names we'll never know. They are domestic workers and farm workers. They are working in factories and they work in restaurants and they're in academia, engineering, medicine, and science. They're part of the world of tech and politics and business. They're our athletes in the Olympics and they're our soldiers in the military.

And there's someone else, Recy Taylor, a name I know and I think you should know, too. In 1944, Recy Taylor was a young wife and mother walking home from a church service she'd attended in Abbeville, Alabama, when she was abducted by six armed white men, raped, and left blindfolded by the side of the road coming home from church. They threatened to kill her if she ever told anyone, but her story was reported to the NAACP where a young worker by the name of Rosa Parks became the lead investigator on her case and together they sought justice. But justice wasn't an option in the era of Jim Crow. The men who tried to destroy her were never persecuted. Recy Taylor died ten days ago, just shy of her 98th birthday. She lived as we all have lived, too many years in a culture broken by brutally powerful men. For too long, women have not been heard or believed if they dare speak the truth to the power of those men. But their time is up. Their time is up.

Their time is up. And I just hope -- I just hope that Recy Taylor died knowing that her truth, like the truth of so many other women who were tormented in those years, and even now tormented, goes marching on. It was somewhere in Rosa Parks's heart almost 11 years later, when she made the decision to stay seated on that bus in Montgomery, and it's here with every woman who chooses to say, "Me too." And every man -- every man who chooses to listen.

In my career, what I've always tried my best to do, whether on television or through film, is to say something about how men and women really behave. To say how we experience shame, how we love and how we rage, how we fail, how we retreat, persevere and how we overcome. I've interviewed and portrayed people who've withstood some of the ugliest things life can throw at you, but the one quality all of them seem to share is an ability to maintain hope for a brighter morning, even during our darkest nights.

So I want all the girls watching here, now, to know that a new day is on the horizon! And when that new day finally dawns, it will be because of a lot of magnificent women, many of whom are right here in this room tonight, and some pretty phenomenal men, fighting hard to make sure that they become the leaders who take us to the time when nobody ever has to say "Me too" again.

Goop Podcast with Gwyneth Paltrow
(2018)

Gwyneth
I am beyond excited to be launching the first episode of the Goop podcast with one of my heroes who not coincidentally happens to be a lot of people's hero, Oprah Winfrey.

Oprah
I believe that fundamentally we are all the same.

Gwyneth
I had to pinch myself a few times during our conversation, talking to Oprah about all the ways she has pushed and continues to push boundaries in her career and life.

Oprah
Don't hold anything too tightly just wish for it. Want it. Let it come from the intention of real truth for you and then let it go. And if it's supposed to be yours it will show up, it won't show up until you stop holding it so tightly.

Gwyneth
As a philanthropist, talk show host, producer, actor, mentor and modern thought leader. Oprah has been instrumental in breaking open old paradigms and paving the way for new voices ideas and movements. I'm so incredibly grateful for the

chance to sit down with her and continue to learn from her. Here she is; Oprah.

Oprah
I'll try not to run the show.

Gwyneth
You can run the show.

Oprah
Actually, there's a very big misconception.
It is not true. I like to surround myself with people who can run things so that I can be free to be with my thoughts.

Gwyneth
How have you gotten there? Because I really do think that to be able to continue to expand and to create you do need time.

Oprah
You can't do it without time.

Gwyneth
How did you get there? Was there a period of time where you felt that you needed to do everything yourself?

Oprah
Yes, including booking the guests and on the Oprah Show when I first started. And then I realized I'm really terrible at

this. But it was really important to me in the beginning to do every job so that I would understand what other people were doing. And obviously I couldn't do the videotape room.

I did no editing because when I first started out in television, the very first day I was sent out on assignment, I was asked if I could edit, even though I couldn't, I said I could. I went to people and said you got to show me how to edit this. This is back in the old days where they're using Bell and Howell film and you had to go in the room and actually cut the little pieces of film.

I would say that this power of my being able to move forward has been based on me paying attention. And Maya Angelou used to say to me all the time, babe, you are where you are because you are obedient to the call. Even when I tell you things, I like the way you listen, and then decide for yourself whether it is for you. And I've been doing that a very long time.

But I actually learned I wasn't just a talk show. I was also a listening show. I feel, Gwyneth, at this particular time in my life, that all of that listening has come to fill a space of knowing for me, that I would not had, had I not actually listened.

Probably you've heard me say over the years, there was a time where it made the shift from it being a show, to it being a ministry, and it being just an expression of myself to the world. And that shift, that ability for me to offer every day, whether it was Tom Cruise or Brad Pitt or a woman who'd lost everything she owned because her husband kicked her out of the house, or victims of abuse, domestic violence kids, whatever the subject. I was able to find the thread of hope in it. I was able to find what is the thing that's going to connect it to the audience.

I'm always looking for what is that thing. How is what you're saying going to resonate with the people who are listening. Because I believe that fundamentally we are all the same, that's why when you go to a movie, you cry, you experience joy, or you have any kind of reaction.
What I started calling aha moments, the aha's are a vibrational frequency that's touching what's already there. That's what makes you go, aha, I knew that I just wasn't able to express it in that way. Aha, that feels familiar, that that sounds right, that feels like the truth to me. That's what an aha is, it's a remembering.

Gwyneth
It's a resonance.

Oprah
It's a resonance and it's a remembering of what you always knew.

Gwyneth
Do you find, especially when you're in your position in this show, that's what people really fee, like so many people don't have the tools to connect to those aha moments.

Oprah
They don't, they sort of are doing their thing, they're busy, their head down. I feel like now we're more in the culture, more open to spirituality and more open to resonance and open-mindedness.

GP
I feel especially during the 80s and 90s, there was more doing than being, and I feel like part of the thing that you did was sort of introduce in a way this spirituality.

OW
I feel that we do too, and I think it's exciting to me that it's catching up to what I knew and believed it could be. But when I first started talking about spirituality, we had a little segment on called; Remembering your Spirit, because I was just trying to get people, little pieces of it.

I remember doing a show with Carolyn Mace who wrote the Anatomy of Spirit and in the middle of that show, I'm watching the audience. I use the audience to gauge the larger world audience, I can tell who's listening, and who's not listening and I could tell the people who just zoned out.

And so I stopped the show, stopped the taping and said; hey are you still with us? A woman stood up and said, no we're not, what are you talking about? Spirit. This was in 92, and I said well you know, mind, body, spirit, right? Because I said you know, you have a body and you have a spirit and she goes, well I know I have a mind of a body but what are you talking about spirit.

In 1992 while we were talking about the anatomy of spirit, people did not know what spirit is. And then somebody else said; are you talking about Jesus Christ? you're talking about disciples? Are you talking about the Bible? What are you talking about? No, I said I'm talking about the part of you that is your essence. That is like your soul. That is the part that never dies. And therefore we have to start from ground zero to explain what the word spirit means. Now we're a long way from that, but I will say that the show, The Oprah Show was a part of opening up that aperture to talk about it, in a way that's not so woo woo. And, of course, when you are pioneering anything, introducing new ideas to the culture, you get criticized.

Gwyneth
You do?

Oprah
Yeah, did you hear that people are resistant to anything that removes them from their current way of thinking. Because it means that I have to let go of who I think I am and make room for the possibility of something else.

Gwyneth
So it's threatening?

Oprah
Yeah, it feels threatening and also like I'm used to doing things the way I've been doing it. And then, if I have to change my belief, I have to believe which is the thing that is fundamentally disruptive to people.

If I have to change what I believe, then it means that I may not be who I think I am. Because I've based who I think I am on a beliefsystem.

I used to always do these shows about not hitting your kids and is spanking ok? So in the 80s we were still having that discussion. Is it ok to spank your kids? And I remember major moment with a viewer in a grocery store saying to me, you changed my life, and I used to just say, oh ok thank you. And then I started stopping to pay attention to what that really meant because when somebody says to you, you change my life that's a major thing. When she said, well I used to beat my kids, and I used to hear you talk every time on TV about don't beat your kids, don't beat your kids. And she said how you going have good kids if you don't beat them?

She said I decided one day I'm going to see. I will try this for one week, I'm not going to beat my kids. So, I did not hit my son for a week and then I tried it another week and I didn't hit my son, and then she said you know it's been 3 weeks now and I haven't hit my son, now I have a different son and I am a different mother. She said it's not because the first time you said it, it's because you were consistent. So, a little change like that, look at the impact on that son on that mother and on that family. I recognized by paying attention, that it's the little things that turn into big things and make major changes in people's lives.

I mean that's a powerful thing that happened because I was consistent. That was a lesson to me, and I paid attention to that. It's important to me to remain consistent in my ideas and consistent in whatever it is I'm trying to offer. That was a life-changing moment for me. Hearing that kind of feedback from someone.

Gwyneth
And how do you hold being that person in the world?

Oprah
Well, I think we are all that person in the world. The difference is through the platform of that show. Because who I am and the world, I have access to more people. But one of the things I said when I was ending the show is everybody has their own platform and their level of influence. I recognize that I am a big soul. You know if you're a big soul, the souls you influence are in direct proportion to the amount of people you're able to affect.

Yeah, that means I'm a big soul. There are smaller souls that are also equally as powerful in their field. Just because you can't reach a lot of people doesn't mean that you don't have the same impact on the people that you are reaching.

I think I value knowing that I don't think of myself as a personality, as much as I think of myself as a being a personality that has come to affect and to influence through my own expression.

One other thing, if I were to do a book, which I keep thinking I might, and then I think it's too hard. I would have to talk about my parents, and I don't want to. I keep doing pieces of books. It would be about these great lessons I learned from listening. I just learned so much from listening. You know I never had a day of therapy, but I had multiple days of therapy by listening and trying to not repeat mistakes that I had conversations about. For a long time, I was taking it in to the point where I was making myself ill. I had to find a way to shield myself from other people's energy, protect myself from it and not take everything in. But also be able to listen.

Gwyneth
And how did you do that?

Oprah
I started to practice in the elevator. First of all, I started meditating.

Gwyneth
What kind?

Oprah
Transcendental meditation.

OPRAH WINFREY

Gwyneth
What's your mantra?

Oprah
I do all forms and you know the greatest meditation for me is actually living. Eckhart Tolle told me this. If you never meditate in your life that being able to live in the present moment is the greatest form of it. When you can just be fully present.
So I started in the elevator going down to do my show having like a moment of covering myself with light, physically having that visualization of covering myself in light, so that I was protected from any harm and also opening myself up to be a vessel that was bigger than my personality.
So that whatever I said, would come from a place of respect and honor, intention and love and in a way that people could feel that. So, one of the biggest changes for me was around 89, 90. I read Zuckoff's book, it was the principle of intention that actually changed my life forever.

Gwyneth
I need to get this book.

Oprah
He has two chapters actually on intention, if I were to say I was brought up Christian I believe in the Christian philosophy, but my true religion is the golden rule which is born of the

third law of motion in physics which says, what you put out is coming back all the time.

For every action there's an equal and opposite reaction. So Zuckoff talked about this in Seat of the Soul. He also talked about this principle of intention that exists always, before there even is a cause or an effect.

There is an intention that creates the cause, you have a reason for wanting to do things. What is the true reason? What is the pure truth of the reason why you're doing a thing? And if you look at what the intention is in every circumstance in your life, the energy of the intention that comes before the cause is automatically going to create an effect. The intention is what actually creates the effect. It is the motivation behind the reason you do the thing that creates the effect.

Gwyneth
So if it's coming from a place of lack or fear?

Oprah
That is going to show up in the effect. When I used this for everything in my life, I stop saying yes when I meant no. I stopped going to places I didn't really want to be. I stop doing things for people I really didn't want to do. Because what happens is I used to have the disease to please. What happens is if you continue to say yes because you want the people to think I'm nice. I don't want them to think that I've got a big head. I don't want them to think I want to. That's exactly what they think, they think you're nice, they think you meant what

you said and that's why they come back. I couldn't understand why I would loan people money, I would do things for them, then they would show up and ask again, why are they asking me again? I just did it.

They're asking you again because your intention was to make them think it's okay to ask. I'm sure I can be your doormat, because you're going to ask me at the last minute to show up for you and I'm going to do it. And so, when I started just doing things based upon what is my intention. That actually changed me. The very first time I got the principle, I used it in my own life to say no to someone really important. He would ask me to do something and I thought normally I would have said yes because I didn't want that person mad at me, and then I just said no I'm not going to do that. It was a benefit to me show up Stevie Wonder. I'm not going to do that. Sorry I can't do that. And he just said okay. I was stunned, I thought it was going to be this big long negotiation. I just said no and saying no as it's been a big thing in my life.

I mean I just recently was in an instance where somebody was asking me to do a benefit for them that I didn't want to do. They wanted me to be honorary chair. I don't put my name on anything that I am notactually involved with. So, if you see my name there, means I did something.
I don't show up unless I feel like this is where I want to be. The person was saying well why wouldn't you do it? In theend you

must love the children, I get that you love the children and it's for the children.

I guess yes I do love the children and I'm taking care of a lot of children, but I don't want to do that. And I actually had to just say, why can't you hear the no way? Why can't you hear the no? I wouldn't have been able to do years ago, I would have just done it, so that person would not be mad at me.

Gwyneth

I think so many of us especially women suffer from that. I mean we all have that disease to please. I certainly do. It's something that I'm really trying to focus on working on at this stage in my life, because you know, on the one hand, I feel the freedom of saying no and drawing a boundary, and, on the other hand, I worry about hurting people's feelings and not being what they thought I was, etc. So how do you what is the practice to get there.

Oprah

Well, what you want is to get this principle of intention, so that everything that you bring to everything you do, comes strong. I talk about frequencies and vibrations all the time, because I think that's what we all are. I think everything, the trees the grass. You are emanating a kind of energy from that you draw to you like energy. You want that energy, your frequency to be the strongest. You know when I finally said yes, I didn't say yes to doing this interview until I could say a full 100 percent yes. I don't want part of me to be sitting in the chair and another part to feel, I should have done that or I should be doing this. I wanted when I can fully say yes, and do it from a space that makes me feel good and not just you feel good.

Gwyneth
Right.

Oprah
Even though you were really persistent.

Gwyneth
Well, there's no other first interview I could have beside you.

Oprah
But you got me with your good Gwyneth, you're good.

Gwyneth
I'm not even Catholic I knew how to guilt you.

Oprah
Yes, I thought ok what would be a reason for me to do so.

Gwyneth
And what was it?

Oprah
First of all, it's your first. And I remember when I was trying to do my very first show how hard it was to get a first. And we

were like bribing Don Johnson because he was doing Miami Vice. We were like doing everything. It's so hard to get that first. I've been there with that first.

Also, I was thinking ok what would I talk about that I haven't said before? And you know then I thought it well I'm really proud of what Ava DuVernay has done with Wrinkle. This is a big moment for Storm and I can talk about them and we can talk about what's going on with women in the you know, in the MeToo. But there are lots of things we can talk about that I thought would be interesting for Goop.

Gwyneth
Also, you know I ran into you at a party recently and I was coming off like a spate of people beating me up for talking about whatever, you know alternative medicine. And you were so encouraging about staying the course and believing in myself.

Oprah
Any time you speak, alternative people are like what does that mean? That's true. I got so beat up with people saying, oh now it's a church of Oprah.

It's the church of Oprah trying to start your own religion. What are you doing and what are you talking about spirit? I just stayed the course. What I realized was, and Marianne told me this, I used to be such a zealot for things, like you've got to get this, oh my gosh you got to know this.

I realized and said to my team, we are our greatest competition. There is no competition other than yourself. Don't worry about what the other guy is doing. You waste energy you take energy away from yourself even if you're in a race, to turn around and see where the other guy is playing.

Gwyneth
I agree.

Oprah
So just focus on what you can do, because you can't beat them at their race. You can only win your own. So during all of those years every time there'd be another show that would come out, my staff would go oh my God, Geraldo Rivera, oh Ricki Lake, oh my God. You know I think there were like 147 talk shows that came up.

And after a while you just learned, they learned, focus focus focus on what it is you want, you can do that better. Do the very best of your ability, because you can't be what somebody else is.
So to answer your other question about how do you get there. Years ago, I have a story for everything because I used to listen to stories for 25 years. One of the most impressive ones was a woman who her son had died of either cancer or AIDS, I don't remember, but she climbed into bed with him as he was taking his last breath and he said his last words, she could barely hear only because she was lying against his chest. He said oh mom,

it was all so simple, so simple. Mom closed his eyes and he died.

I got chills when I heard it. It's one of those things that resonates as an aha, I said we're making it all so complicated and it's really all so simple. That was also a big life changing moment for me. How am I making it more complicated than it needs to be. How can I slow down pay attention, and see the simplicity in things and sort of follow these laws that I've come to know to be true. The universal language that all human beings and all of nature is speaking.
I started to practice actually what I know to be true. I say that to everyone who's listening to us right now, you already know and you may have God as a guide or inspiration, the reason why you're drawn to that. You're the reason why people are drawn to those inspirations. There is something there that is yearning to remember, yearning to be reminded.
Gwyneth
That's beautifully said.

Oprah
The beauty that you hold of the experiences and adventures you want to share, the love you want to offer. The expression you want to give. What does this remind you in physical form in tangible ways and in non-tangible ways are pieces of yourself that are beautiful and that want to aspire to the best. We're all just trying to reach for the highest truest expression of ourselves as human beings. That's the commonality that we

share. And the thing that I know is, whether I meet someone on skid row or meet someone sitting in a billionaire's club, that person wants the same thing. They want to be able to have what is the fullest truest expression of themselves as a human being.

And how do you do that? You know you can't get there without practice, without being connected to the essence of yourself to the source of your creation, it is like developing a spiritual muscle. It does not happen if you're just running around all the time. So just like you bathe to stay clean and wash your hair and brush your teeth, are practices that keep yourself healthy and viable. There are also spiritual practices that do the same and transcendental meditation is one of them.

It is one of the practices but for me, a conscious working model is to stay fully present here and now. I practice it if I'm at thesink and putting a cup in the sink. I'm walking down the stairs and walking up the stairs, I am in that moment conscious of my hand is on the railing.

Gee one foot is in front of the other, wow my legs are moving every day. This has happened for all the years of my life. I can't believe my body is still functioning this way. Isn't this great?

Bathing is my hobby, I'm putting the bath salts in the water, I'm lighting the candle. I'm aware of that, I'm fully just there, I'm just there. I'm experiencing the water my tub happens to sit in a place where I get to see the ocean. I was in the water looking at the white caps on the ocean, I'm like wow.

Every part of it is beauty to me. Brings a little piece of joy and helps my frequency. I'm doing that all the time, I'm doing that even if something shows up that is uncomfortable. You know who taught me that? Its Maya Angelou. Because I lived as you have lived every other week in the tabloids.

And every time I would get so upset about it, Maya would say but baby, you don't have anything to do with that, they're saying it and you know it's not true. It has nothing to actually do with you. It has to do with whoever sat down at the computer at that moment. You know it's been happening for so long. She actually said whoever's sitting at the typewriter they're thinking what can we say this week that's going to sell some stories?
It's also why I stopped making as many public appearances with Stedman, because I realized that every time there's a new photograph there's a new story.

Gwyneth
Who was Maya to you?

Oprah
She was in many ways the embodiment in physical form of what this character which I will talk about later, that I'm now portraying in a Wrinkle In Time. This celestial wise through millennia angel woman. She was the mother figure for me.

You know my biological mother didn't have the opportunity to be educated. Being raised in the south being a domestic worker her whole life, she didn't have the opportunities, that Maya Angelou so fortunately had been exposed to. So my mother couldn't give me what Maya had. I needed a mother to mentor me through this whole fame process.

And so she was my grounding tool for it all. I learned my greatest lessons from her. She was my comfort she was my nurturer she was my inspiration. She was the person who was saying you can do it babe you can do it. And she'd say take it all the way. And then she would point to the stars, take it all the way. Go all the way.

Even now when something goes very right or something goes very wrong, her spirit abides with mine. And I verbally call on her.

Gwyneth
Out loud.

Oprah
Out loud. Like when I woke this morning, I said Maya going to be doing this interview with Gwenyth and show up.

Gwyneth
And here she is.

Oprah
And here she is. Yes, I mean Maya, I'm going to be, you know why? Because I feel that there is a responsibility that comes when you are speaking to millions of people. There is a responsibility that comes with that.

You owe that some thought, you owe that to just not be. It's why I'm very very careful on social media. I don't think that it's the best forum for expressing the deepest parts of yourself and so I'm careful about what I say and what I don't say, and how it can be interpreted because I think words matter, and have such great power, lasting power.

I think about it, I think about just as before I would do for every show. I would empty myself and say let me be a vessel for something bigger than I am, because I know I'm speaking to lots of crazy people who can interpret whatever we're doing or saying in whatever way they want.

So let the crazies hear this carefully, lots of people who are in need and lots of people who are just open to hear what you have to say, and people who are not. Let me be a vessel for something that's bigger than myself.

Gwyneth
And when you say, there's a responsibility in it. What does that mean to you?

Oprah
I mean to me, it means that I think every person who comes to earth has a responsibility to just seek the truest highest expression, and the key word here is true responsibility. How do you not just speak the truth? How are you the truth? Responsibility is to show up in that which is the most authentic truthful version of yourself. That's how I see it.

Gwyneth
I think that you know when you were talking about Maya Angelou, what she was to you, without sounding completely cheesy, that's what you are to so many of us.

Oprah
Well, that would mean, if I could open to it, if I could see that, I don't know. I wouldn't be able to bear that. I couldn't. I don't know what that would mean. I don't.

Gwyneth
It's true, though.

Oprah
Ok, I don't know what that would mean.

Gwyneth
And you somehow gave us all permission to seek that well, that's good.

Oprah
Well, that's a good life.

Gwyneth
That space wasn't there for us before you named it and you gave us all permission.

Oprah
Really.

Gwyneth
Yeah.

Oprah
I'm going to think about that.

Gwyneth
Ok.

Oprah
After you leave it and take me a minute.

Gwyneth
That's fine.

Oprah
I would say though that this thing of "Oh mom it's so simple," that the reason why people's lives get so complicated is

because you're trying to live it for somebody else other than yourself.

That is the key. Make it simple. When you just start doing it for yourself. And that is not a selfish thing. That is an honorable thing. I remember in the 90s I had Cheryl Richardson on who is a life coach. We were doing this test in the audience and asking women where are you on the list of 10 years, 10 priorities, the 10 top things that you prioritize. Most of the women in the audience, it was around 92 93 did not have themselves on the list or they were at the bottom of the list. And when Sheryl said out loud, you should be first on the list, they started booing in the Oprah Show audience and I had to say, I remember it so vividly, I'm saying hey we're not Jerry Springer here.

Gwyneth
Wow.

Oprah
In the mid 90s people were like, are you kidding? And that women are shouting. She doesn't have children, so how does she know? I said, she didn't say abandon your children and leave them in the street, she said put yourself on the list so you can better take care of your children. Well, that principle of not being selfish but self-aware enough to honor the vessel the vehicle that is your body, that is your way on earth.

Your presence here on Earth in this dense form, there is nothing more important than that, because what you give and feed to yourself that makes yourself whole, creates an opportunity to have your cup overflows to give more to other people. You can only do that at your best when you've come from a whole place.

Gwyneth
Right. Do you feel whole?

Oprah
Yeah, I really do.

Gwyneth
Are you happy?

Oprah
Oh happiness is not even a word I use for myself. Cause happiness seems temporal, it builds temporary, these things happen. I'm so happy now. It is far deeper than happiness. I can get happy about things, but I'm generally in such a state of quiet contentment.

Beneath the surface of whatever it is, and in a sense of peace about things that happiness is sort of like an afterthought. Of course, I'm happy. Of course, I'm happy because I'm basically at peace and content. I've talked to over 37,000 people, but I've also listened.

I see the commonality in my experiences with other people. I live a very luxurious highly elevated life. I have always loved beauty and being surrounded by beauty. So, to now be in a place that I live, in a place that's like a park to me.

Well, before I had oak trees surrounded by flower gardens, I lived in a little apartment in Baltimore, and I couldn't afford any art. I would go to the art museum and buy postcards of Monet and Manet, Picasso and Klimt and I would frame the postcards on the wall.

Gwyneth
That's amazing.

Oprah
To me that was my art. And then when I could start to like buy little pieces like Beurden sketches or you know move into the world where you can actually spend money on some art. The very first important piece now and still is the most important, though not most expensive in my home, is a picture of a slave woman on the auction block with her daughter.
When you come in my house, it is the first thing you see. That is the grounding painting for me. Then there's the first major piece I bought like back in 1988.

Gwyneth
Who painted it?

OPRAH WINFREY

Oprah

A guy named Harry Roselyn who is a 19th-century genre painter who painted a lot of black folks, but that woman whom I've named Ana and her daughter Sarah, I don't even know their particular story, but I know their story.

And one of the other things that I treasure in my home, I have documents from slave plantations that have the names and ages and prices of slaves, and sometimes when I feel like there have been times when I've been in crisis or felt like things weren't going the way I wanted them to go. I will go into that room and I will speak their names out loud. Douglass and Jenna and Carrie and Sarah and Anna and their ages and their prices and remind myself of how far I have come, and no crisis seems that much of a crisis after you look at the names, the ages, the prices of people who were before you. Who made this way possible. So that's actually how I live my life. It sounds like whew, but it really is. Really, it really is.

I say this to my beautiful South African daughters when we're around the table. You should actually pay attention, the reason you should pay attention is because I was lucky enough to get you when you were 12 years old, and I have no agenda other than your highest well-being.

I don't need you as a reflection of me, I don't have that parenting thing. You've got to do well because it makes me look good. I just have your highest well-being as my only agenda. That's the only thing I'm looking out for. Anything I ask or anything I tell, I have really great relationships with them.

Gwyneth
That's crazy you know, it just occurred to me when you said that. I mean when people talk about or strive to be a mother like that, to me it is the ideal characteristic of a mother.

Oprah
I just want what's the highest for you.

Gwyneth
And it's so difficult.

Oprah
To not get attached to the other?

Gwyneth
Exactly, and not project and not see your own shortcomings in your kid and get triggered by it.

Oprah
We want you to be something that's going to reflect back to me, so it's a good thing.

Gwyneth
This is very tough, we were all raised so much with that kind of enmeshed way with our parents and that is the most profound. It's so funny, because you're technically not a mother. And that is the most profound and insightful sentence about mothering. I mean in terms of you just really crystallize something for me there.

Oprah
I'm glad it's one of the reasons why I could do it from the age of 12. I was also self-aware enough even when there was all this pressure to get married, like you should get married and you should have children so that our children could grow up together. Well, that's not a reason, I got to tell you. It would be nice, but not a reason.

Gwyneth
Talking about the intention behind something.

Oprah
I didn't think Maya had said this to me, that her mother was not a good mother for small children. That she was raised by her grandmother was one of the reasons we connected so well, because I was raised by my grandmother the first six years. She was raised by her grandmother in the south and her mother was not a good mother for smart young children, but her mother was a great mother for her as a young adult woman.

Her mother could relate to her as an adult woman and so she later forgave her mother for not being there for her as a child. They became really strong. I had a really strong bond till the end, but I don't think I would have been a good mother for baby children. Cause I need you to talk to me and I need you to tell me what's wrong, I can't just figure it out.
I always knew that about myself, always better with kids once they turned two and a half three. I had a real resonance with them and was like, oh you love babies and babies are fine, so I don't think that was for me. Even when people were saying but you could have your own nursery and you could build it in Harpo.

It didn't feel like it was for me, so I was searching even for that. What is the higher ground for me? Where will I be able to find my instinct for nurturing, caring and support for other people? Where and how will that show up for me?

Gwyneth
I do want to talk to you about twothings. One, is this seismic change in what's happening with regards to women in this country? The MeToo movement and why now. Why do you think now?

Oprah
Well, you can look at any given moment, one of my favorite books on earth. If you're going to be a human being, you need to read a New Earth by Eckhart Tolle.

OPRAH WINFREY

Gwyneth
Is someone writing this down?

Oprah
Okay you have to read a New Earth by Eckhart Tolle. The first chapter is a little slow and you think, what is this really. By the time you get to the second chapter about the ego and the third chapter about the roles that you play vs your ego, and then the fifth chapter on the body pain that so many people carry, you begin to get it.
What he says, is how do you know you're supposed to be experiencing any given thing in any moment. The reason you know, is because you're experiencing that thing. So, if it's happening, it's supposed to be happening, right?

How you manage that, is understanding that there is nothing showing up that isn't supposed to teach you something about your own personal life, and it's teaching you about your own personal life to the direct extent that you are involved in it, and it's teaching us something about our entire consciousness.

It is the thing that I have come to know for sure, is that there is no experience that you can have personally, or that we can have as a body of consciousness. This culture isn't here to help strengthen or elevate us. You can use everything to take you to higher ground. This moment has been coming for a very long time, that's what I was trying to say in my Golden Globes speech that I wasn't trying to run for any office.

I wanted to be able to say to the MeToo movement, Proud of where we are, what we're doing, but you need to know you didn't get here alone, there are those who endured, suffered, didn't speak because they couldn't speak, because they knew that to speak would mean I won't be able to feed my children, and who has come before you that made this path possible. So, it's been coming for a very long time. That's what the Recy Taylor story.

Gwyneth
Why does it have traction? Because I think, now I look back and I think throughout modern media, women have come forward about this person or that person or X Y and Z.

Oprah
It has traction for the same reason that the kids in Florida now have traction. Look at how many people had to die in order for that to get traction. I thought it was going to happen for sure to Sandy Hook. That was actually my first thought when I heard there had been a shooting and a five-year-old had been killed. I thought this will be the thing, this will be the one that breaks down. This will be the breakthrough, this will get us to change. It's only because it happened with Harvey.
They were known to people, people had some kind of connection to something. There was a resonance, a feeling of vibration whatever you want to call it. That's number one. Number two, it had been coming with Cosby and nothing happened, they had been coming with Bill O'Reilly, had been

coming even with the president of the United States, where people can hear the Access Hollywood tape and yet nothing happens.

It had been coming. And so that moment was the moment where it all crystallized. It's just like everybody's so excited as I, about the phenomenon, that is a black panther. Black Panther couldn't have happened 10 years ago. The way it happened recently is because in order for phenomena to be a phenomenon, everything has to line up.

It means the culture, the zeitgeist for this particular moment in time, ready, available and open to hear that message. And so, it took woman after woman unheard, unspoken and now some faces come forward that we recognize and have some resonance with.

My God, it could happen to them, than this thing that I've been hiding within myself, that I was so ashamed of, that I felt guilty about, because I'm just a waitress or a nurse or a clerk or a secretary or an assistant or whatever. Wow if it could happen to them. That really means something.

The resonance happens because there's been enough puncturing of the veil in the culture, that finally is large enough for people to hear it. Now, I will use this philosophy from my show days. But even as a young reporter I started to figure this out, that I hated being in the newsroom.

It just felt like I was in the wrong space in my life, and I was always asking God where am I supposed to be really? But now I realize, oh I needed that. So as a young reporter in Baltimore, I started to notice I was the street, I was assigned togo out on the street whenever anything happened, so I'm just literally in the car with the photographer. I'd get sent to the ambulance accidents and everything and there came a time where when I first started at 22, if there was a drunk driving accident, that would be in front of the news. After a while you'd have to kill more than one person.

A child had to be involved, and then they had to be more children before it could make the front of the news, we would go further and further and further back in the news because it was just so common. I remember one night, I was working late and there was a school bus accident where seven children coming from choir practice doing Christmas carols were killed by a drunk driver, that made the front of the news.

I thought oh that's where we are now. You've got to be seven kids coming from a choir practice singing Christmas carols to get people's attention. I started to learn from that, that the culture becomes numb, they can't hear it. And then finally there is a massive enough number, a critical mass that people can hear it. I'm certainly willing to support and get behind these kids in Florida feel like the new freedom writers to me.

Gwyneth
And that's the difference between Sandy Hook.

Oprah
And those were little kids.

Gwyneth
These young men and women have voices and power.

Oprah
Their parents tried to have power, but they tried to do it in such a diplomatic quiet way, that they were shut down. Can you believe that parents of little 5-and-6-year-olds go to Congress and cannot be heard? It makes no sense, but that's why I'm willing to get behind these kids who feel like the new day is on the horizon. For this moment in time women can be heard. In this moment in time, the young voices can be heard. The reason why it excites me so much about the young people in Florida is because they're going to take the energy and power of that pain and turn it into something miraculous.

I know what that means when you use those deaths to actually turn it into something. Seventeen people were killed, I believe death is here to show us more about how to live. I felt this after 9/11. We had it for a moment and then we lost it. Those people were sacrificial angels allowing us to look at ourselves in a different way and our country, our culture and the way we operated in the world. The same thing is true for this moment in time, I believe for the children in Florida who are rising up, who've said enough.

OPRAH WINFREY

Gwyneth
The culture of enough.

Oprah
Yes, the culture of enough with the same thing for the women.

Gwyneth
Do you have any practical advice? This is something that we're talking about a lot in the office right now because of so many women when the MeToo movement started. It's sort of everybody. I don't have one friend, one colleague, one school mother who wasn't either sexually harassed sexually abused molested. Not one.

Oprah
It touched everybody obviously there's a spectrum, there's a lot now. Women were all talking about experiences, and obviously there's healing in that. But I think we're all a little bit stuck on how did you heal from sexual abuse?
Well, that is a process. But I will tell you this, knowing that you're not alone is a part of the big healing. I remember the first time I realized that I wasn't the only kid who had been sexually molested, the first time I realized that I was doing a talk show where somebody was telling their story.
I was like dumbfounded, I didn't know what to do. That is my story. This is a good cry right now. I was like, has this happened to someone else? I thought I was the only one, the first time I heard it I was in Baltimore and I didn't have the courage to

speak out on television about it. I had a cohost in the girls telling the story and I'm like that's just like me. That sounds like me. It was her uncle. Oh my gosh. She was the same age. Oh my gosh.

Afterwards I went into the greenroom and I said it to her, she said why didn't you say something? I said, I never heard that it ever happened to anybody before and I don't know. I don't know what the truth was, I was scared.
I was 22 or 23 at the time and that's when I started to realize, oh this has happened to somebody before. So, when it happened on television, when I was the master of my own show, I said I'm not going to let this moment pass.

And I said, MeToo, on the air to that girl, and she was like, were you? Yes, I said. And then it started this whole thing. But the power comes in being able to say, first of all, it did happen, because a lot of women tell themselves it was something else. I just wrote what I know for sure, for the magazine about this. At the time, I was being sexually harassed in my years in Baltimore, there were several years where I had a boss who just did it, and I didn't say anything. I don't hold any guilt about it, I also don't hold any guilt about not speaking up as a child.
I would say you speak up when you feel that you are safe enough to speak up, you tell and tell and tell until there's someone who will believe you. Whether you were a child or whether you're an adult, you can get support and feel safe.

The reason I didn't tell as a child when I was being sexually molested by one person is because I knew I would be blamed.

I knew that it would somehow turn on me and it would make my life worse, make that person then turns on the whole family. I didn't know if I'd be harmed. So, I didn't feel safe. I would say to anyone even now, if you're in an environment where you have a situation where you're being harassed, you speak up where you can feel safe to speak up, and that you're not going to be retaliated against, in a way that is going to cause you more harm. I would speak to that person directly, I think what the MeToo movement has done is give women the power to say, back off.

Gwyneth
Right, it was interesting to me to see all of the men when this all happened. Taking such forensic inventory of how they had behaved and somebody could have construed this the wrong way to say the wrong thing. You know men who won't be accused of anything. Taking inventory.

Oprah
Those are the people doing the real inventory. Like have I said anything or done anything? Or have I crossed the line? I'm sure a lot of men have, because we live and have lived in a culture that allowed you to cross the line. So, lots of lines have been crossed and now it's up to both women and men to redefine where those lines are. I think we're in this moment

of figuring it out. And that's really ok yeah. We're figuring it out.

Gwyneth
I don't think we like that as a culture. I think we like things binary they should be good or bad, right or wrong.

Oprah
That's right.

Gwyneth
We're living in a time now where we're having to really embrace the gray areas explore them, and kind of come together and figure out. Are we redrawing lines? What does that mean? And it's ok that it feels confusing for a minute.

Oprah
For a minute. But I think that clarity is on the way, and I think that the fact that this movement has given every woman in every part of the globe a deepened and heightened sense of, I can stand up for myself.

Gwyneth
Right.

Oprah
I can push back without feeling like I'm going to be harmed is an important part of this phase of the movement. Yeah, but

we're on our way. We're on our way to something bigger. But you know what, it's what's even more important. The sexual harassment sexual assault.

I had people online saying, oh I knew about Harvey, I should have known. Well, first of all, I wasn't in this world. I was in Chicago in my own little world. But my point is this, what I knew about Harvey was that Harvey was a bully and that if he was on the phone, you didn't want to take the call because you're going to get bullied in some way. For me, it just meant pushing for some people to be on the show that I didn't want to, and I've already done it, how many more times we need to do so? That's all I knew about Harvey, and I was friendly with him.

Yes, I was friendly with Harvey, I was in association with him for the Butler movie that we had done. But of course, I didn't know of what was going on.

But what I do know is what this moment is here to show us. What I do question for myself is I was willing to put up with the bullying thing.

I was willing to put up with, ok I'll take the call, ok I'll be another, ok I'll do that. And so, it's caused me to question, and I think what this movement will eventually lead us to, is not accepting any kind of behavior that disparages you as a human being, period.

What am I willing to be? Why am I willing to put up with an asshole? The big question is who will accept you as an asshole. We won't tolerate other things, you can throw phones and you can call people jerks, you can do all the nasty stuff but we're not willing to put up with it.

I'm hoping it leads us to a better way for all human beings to treat each other. This movement is leading us towards that, saying not only am I not going to take your sexual harassment, I'm not going to take any of your bullshit, period. I think we're on our way there, I think we're figuring it out.

Gwyneth
When you were acting, did you experience any of that? Or was it only in the newsroom?

Oprah
No, you know why? When you have the power to speak up for yourself. He's not going to say anything to you.

Gwyneth
I didn't when he did it to me. No, I wasn't.

Oprah
So let me ask you this, when this first started to come out. Was there a part of you that was like whoa?

Gwyneth
Very, and it's been months of me trying to process through it all. I think that I came out about Harvey early in the trajectory

of the whole story, I didn't feel safe to do it, but I felt I had a responsibility to do it.

It was clear to me what had happened to me, and it only happened one time. I confronted him and he never tried anything like that again. But he was a bully. So about work things, he was shaming, he was really hard on me. And then he was incredibly generous, he would send me a private plane somewhere and it was kind of a typical abusive relationship.

I don't think that I had started to process through, because so much of my acting career and so many of the incredible highs and lows as well, were associated with him and Miramax, it's brought up a lot of stuff lately, a lot of abuse from my own childhood that I haven't reconciled, which is why I was asking you about that. When you have these moments in your life, where there are all these confluences of events, I started to think, gosh I wonder if that's why I stepped away from acting when I had my child, because I had always told myself the story, I lost the passion for it.

My daughter and I wanted to be home. And now I'm sort of trying to put the pieces together and think, did this predominant relationship in my professional life lead me to not want to do it anymore.

Oprah

Well, certainly it had an influence. I mean certainly, going back to this whole thing of energy and vibrations, you know how you feel when you have to be in a space with someone who is an agitating force. What it means to have to work with that.

You reach a point in your life where you think, I don't want to have to deal with that. I do know that that's how I felt every time I had to be like, oh gosh, you had to get on the phone with that, you got to be around, you had to deal with that.

Gwyneth
Yeah.

Oprah
I'm sure that, that is a component, an element of it. Because if it was a purely joyful experience, where you just get to open up and be your full self all the time, who doesn't want to embrace that? But if there's agitation and negative energy, then there's some dark side stuff in there.

And so, when I feel safe, that's when I talk about speaking up, I'm talking about particularly for children because I've done so many interviews with kids who told, and then they were kicked out of the house and then were abandoned. So, you got to find the place where you feel safe.

That's why this moment in time, where women who didn't know what was going to happen had the courage. That's what courage is, that moment when you're scared but you leave anyway. You're scared but you're going to stand out there anyway. You're going to say it anyway, because you've had enough.

Gwyneth
Also, I had enough for potentially my daughter this whole next generation of women. I just thought this is not us anymore. We can't do this anymore.

Oprah
What I do know for sure, what I do believe really in the deepest part of my spirit, is that our daughters your daughter, my girls. Oh no, they are not going this way. I see my girls now, they are just not going to take it. They're like what, you let somebody say that to you when you were 22? Yeah, I did, in order to keep my job, and I would try to walk around the other way and hold my head down at the desk. That isnot going to happen, that's over.

So, it's the story of this wonderful adventure of this young girl, whose father is a scientist and has been experimenting with how to touch hands with the universe and ends up being zapped out into outer space. She loses her father and he's been missing for four years. And these three angelic forces come to help her find her father who is out there and being taken over by the dark side. It's her journey to find her father, but the journey is also about discovering herself and learning to look at herself as an empowered being. A girl in school where kids are teasing you and all that.

So, it's about that and I get to play the wise Mrs. Which, and Reese is Mrs. Whatsit and Mindy Reese Witherspoon and

Mindy Callum is Mrs. Who, So, there are the three wise women who help her along the journey.

And mine is a millennial force who is a combination for me in my mind of my two favorite mentors Glenda the Good Witch and Maya Angelou. So, it's the embodiment of the wisdom of Maya and the magic of Glenda. And you know it's opening in a couple of days.

Gwyneth

So why did you say yes?

Oprah

I said yes, because Ava DuVernay is a visionary filmmaker whom I had come to know after shooting The Butler with David Oyelowo, who handed me a DVD of her movie Middle of Nowhere.

I watched the movie, I liked it. She shot the movie, made the movie with $200,000 and I googled her. I saw this lovely woman in dreads with her glasses, pretty warm brown face smiling, I thought I'm going to be your friend. I'm going to be her friend. And I ended up having a luncheon here, just so I could meet her. I had a Mother's Day luncheon and said everybody bring your mother just so I could meet her. Because I wasn't going like to call and say I'm going to be your friend.

And we started talking I ended up going on as a producer for Salma, I feel about her the way I believe Maya felt about me. She's this young visionary who has lots of things to say in the world.

I can feel her essence in her spirit rising in her directorial abilities and her advocacy abilities. I just want to support her in every way.

Gwyneth
And she needs you?

Oprah
She doesn't need me. But we've become really good friends, so this is a thing that happened. She was talking about this movie she was doing, and I said oh well you know you're going to be filming in New Zealand? I want to come. I am going to take two weeks off and I'm going to come to New Zealand because I've been there before, and I didn't really get to explore. So, I'm going to come to New Zealand, I'm going to watch you film and just hang out.
And she said well, if you're going to do that, I wanted to ask you, would you read it for this role of Mrs. Which, would you? Why don't you just act?
I said, all right I'll take a look at it. And when I read it, I thought well I am Mrs. Which, you're going to get to play Mrs. Which. And so that's how it came to be.

Gwyneth
Do you like acting? You're really, really good at it.

Oprah
Well, thank you.

OPRAH WINFREY

Gwyneth
I love you as an actress.

Oprah
I don't feel that I'm great at it.

Gwyneth
Really?

Oprah
No, I really don't.

Gwyneth
The Color Purple?

Oprah
I thought I was great in The Color Purple, you know because I was carried by passion.

Gwyneth
You are so good in that movie.

Oprah
The Color Purple is the best story on earth. I mean I never wanted anything more than I wanted The Color Purple, it was the embodiment of the allowing of something to come into your life. I never wanted anything more than I wanted The

Color Purple, and have not since allowed myself to want anything that badly, because I know how not to want it that badly. I know that when you want it so badly that you hurt for it, that you're not going to get it, that it's only through the disallowing of it. When I learned this lesson that not to hold anything too tightly. Just wish for it, want it, let it come from the intention of real truth for you, and then let it go. If it's supposed to be yours it will show up, it won't show up until you stop holding it so tightly. And that's the way you live your life. That's my deep prayer for everyone who's listening to us, that the forces that we call God, nature, universal energy, divine light by every name that is called God in the universe. My prayer is that that force field holds you in the palm of its hands and never squeezes you too tightly.

Gwyneth
Amazing, this has been one of the biggest honors of my life to talk to you.

Oprah
Thank you for saying that.

Gwyneth
I just adore you.

OPRAH WINFREY

Speech at Women's E3 Summit at the Smithsonian
(2018)

Announcer: If there is ever an icon, she is one, through the award-winning Oprah Winfrey Show, she gave voice to people and to issues, rarely seen on television. She made conversations that shaped how generations of Americans thought about themselves and thought about their country. I also want to say publicly that there's so much I could say about her and what she's accomplished. But I want you to know that without the support, without the vision, without the friendship of Oprah Winfrey, there might not be a National Museum of African-American History and Culture.
She may not remember, but years ago like 2005, when we began this endeavor and we were dreaming, we didn't know exactly what to do. She took the time to help shape our dreams, to remind us how to engage a public, how to tell stories that are meaningful and true. She took the time and made a dream a reality, her steadfast support and commitment to the museum have been a source of inspiration for us all, for which we are truly grateful. So, I am really pleased to say this for the first time. Join me in welcoming to the Oprah Winfrey Theater, Miss Oprah Winfrey.

Oprah: Well children where there is so much racket, there's bound to be something out of kilter. I think the women in the north and the men in here, wide bands are going to be in a fixed pretty soon. That little man in the back over there say, women need to be helped into carriages and over mud puddles, and I'm here to tell you ain't nobody helped me into no carriages and I ain't never been helped over nary a mud puddle. And ain't I a woman? Look at me. Look at my arms, I done planted and plowed and gathered into bonds and worked as much as any man would. When I could get it, ain't nobody could hit me and ain't I a woman? I'd done born 13 children, 13 children and seen them all sold off into slavery. And when I cried out with a woman's grief, ain't nobody, but Jesus heard me. And ain't I a woman? I done borne the lashes well, and ain't I a woman?

It's impossible to stand in this space, to be in this building and not feel the spirits. Can you feel them? Have a seat. I want you to have a seat and feel the spirits, feel the spirits, the presence of the spirits who honor us by accepting our invitation to make their homes here in the National Museum of African-American History and Culture. Feel the spirits, because they have waited a very long time to tell their stories. But I wanted to start with the words of Sojourner Truth, because those words, I've been reciting those words out loud since I was a little girl. Somewhere inside myself, I knew that I had come from a long lineage. So I started learning Fannie Lou Hamer, and Sojourner Truth, all the black poets, Maya Angelou. But I've been reciting those words out loud because they resonated so deeply within me.

Because her question, ain't I a woman, is at the heart of why the work to include African-American women's voices in our historical and cultural narrative. In the telling and retelling of each and every story is so absolutely necessary, if we want to be serious about getting to the heart of the matter of gender equality and empowerment in this country. I am honored today, to stand as Oprah Winfrey in the Oprah Winfrey Theater, to add my voice to the choir. So, Sojourner's Truth, her famous question came in response to a definition of womanhood, that had just been offered by a white male delegate to the 1851 Women's Convention in Akron, Ohio. They were doing the same thing in 51 that we're doing here today.

It was a definition which seemed at the time, determined to exclude her altogether. So, rejecting the notion from that little man in the back over there, that wealth, that male protection and that class privilege are what defines who is a woman and who is not. She offers instead her own lived reality as the proof that she needs to take her place and her seat at the welcome table. As she speaks, her passion and her eloquence are undeniable, but here's the thing all these years in reciting that "Ain't I a Woman" speech, in talking to audiences in sharing that story. The thing that is undeniable for me and has impressed me is her certainty. It's her certainty I admire most. It is her defiant refusal to be made less than the woman fully grown that she knows herself to be.
That is what she is asking of all of us, because her woman ness is never up for debate. Ain't I a woman? Her question is actually rhetorical, it's a challenge to little man in the back

over there, and to anyone who thought that they could confine a being as majestic and as magical, as mysterious, as complete as she was, to a small dark space where she could be disrespected and be desexed. Where she could be robbed of her humanity, not a woman, certainly not a man, but some strange, unformed creature distinguished only by her physical strength, by her ability to bear the lash and her ability to suffer the pain of her loss children without going completely mad. I think about her, I think about them all the time. I think about how is it that they did not go insane really.

Again and again and again, and again and again, losing your mother, losing your brother, losing your children, losing your husband. Working all day in the field, getting up before the sun came up, not finishing till the sun went down. Toiling in the hot sun, not being able to ask for a glass of water. Coming home, not just tired, bone tired, exhausted, tired in your bones and your family is gone. Without a word, without a whisper, they are gone. Disappeared, just gone. Come back from the fields and they are just gone. So, hear the words of Alice Walker, when she says, "What is real is what did happen. What happened to me and what happens to me is the most real of all," she says. I'm here to testify that what happened to them is a part of me. It's a part of us. It's a part of me and ain't I a woman?

That question is at the heart of black women's collective experience. It isn't that we haven't tried to answer it. It isn't that we haven't tried, we have. But because it's often just us talking to us about us, because we are often the only people listening when we are talking to us about us. It's been difficult for us to be heard, but not anymore. Not anymore because we have the National Museum of African American History and Culture. I'm here to tell you that it's very creation, it's very existence, it being here screams hear me. Hear me now! Hear me. The words of Mary Helen Washington, she says, "If there is a single distinguishing feature of the literature of black women and this accounts for their lack of recognition it is this that our literature is about us. It's about black women." "It takes the trouble to record the thoughts and the words and the feelings and the deeds and experiences that make the reality of being black in America look very different from what men have written."

Because there is this overall narrative really, but there's also the specific, black woman narrative without which the entire edifice is a lie. No matter how carefully constructed, no matter how carefully presented, as if it contains the truth, the whole truth and nothing but the truth. It does not and cannot because if we are not there, if we are not there, the true American story cannot be told. Because we are always there, and we have always been there doing everything. Being everything, doing our part and then some. Because as Gwendolyn Brooks said, "We would have to conduct our blooming," she said, "In the noise and whip of the whirlwind," that's what she said. So, we did and so we still do. In fact, we're just getting started conducting our business because we've got entrepreneurs and educators and directors and filmmakers and communications, experts, and visionaries. We got first ladies and fearless wars, we got poets, we got politicians, we even got a princess and we've also got our OWN network. And ain't I a woman?

On the OWN network right now, we're focused on telling stories well, so that you can see yourself in them. Stories like Queen Sugar and stories like Greenleaf. On June 19th, Mara Brock Akil brings a new story called Love Is, where you just get to see beautiful, beautiful faces on screen. Beautiful reflections, all of them of art imitating life as we know it. Life in our churches and life in our kitchens and life in our bedrooms. We've been unseen for so long. We've been silent for too long and make no mistake about this, there's a high price to be paid for accepting your own invisibility. There is a diminishing of soul and spirit when the pictures you see and the definitions you hear never reflect your specific womanness. When the truth of who you are is denied relentlessly, aggressively, audaciously. I mean I grew up, there was nobody on the screen, but Buckwheat, nobody wanted to be Buck.

Is it any wonder that we sometimes fell silent and that, that silence created a void. A sense of primal abandonment and despair sometimes, that has shaped not only our history, but has too often shaped our daily lives. Because it makes us the fact that you never see yourself, you never hear your stories. It makes you begin to doubt ourselves, to wonder if we're lacking some elusive, intangible thing that could make us whole. It makes you feel isolated, it makes you be confused, and you begin to wonder if you'll ever be enough? Well, this is what I know after thousands and thousands of interviews, everybody feels that. It's the human condition, am I enough? But it's the human condition on steroids for black women everywhere. You know when I talk to my young girl students in South Africa, the insecurity and the fear that comes up over and over and over for them, is that question, am I enough? Am I enough? Can I be enough?

My answer is always yes, you already are enough, because you come from what is more than enough and you just need to be reminded of where you've come from. That's what this place does, it's why I love this museum so much. It's here to shake the memory banks. It's here to reiterate the knowledge of what you have been through so you know what you can get through. Here the words of Pearl Cleage, she says, "We have sometimes shivered at the edges of a very cold place, where people do not always see our beauty or understand the rhythm of our song." That's what she said, but we never stopped singing. No, how could we? Because in the face of all that attempted silencing, the woman who survives intact must be ever vigilant. She must constantly remind herself that her values and your choices are important. You must know inside in the deepest part of your being that you matter. Not just that you matter, but also why.

So, for me, the foundational base of empowerment, of entrepreneurship, of any kind of engagement, the foundational base of my success, of my wellbeing, my wholeness, my everything is knowing who I am and where I come from. In my living room right now, is a painting that I've owned now for 30 years. You can Google it, it's called "To the Highest Bidder," and it's at the center of my house. It's at the center of my house because it actually is symbolic of the foundation of not the house, but the foundation for my life. The painting is by Harry Roseland, who was a genre painter in the early 20th, late 19th century. The painting's over six feet tall and it shows a slave woman on the auction block, holding her daughter's hand. I cannot come in the door, my front door, or I cannot leave without passing that painting. I am reminded of where I come from every day of my life, and I am reminded because I never want to forget it.

In my library, I have a framed list of in slaved African-American people, remember I showed you. Who were held in bondage on various plantations, listed in the ledgers alongside the cows and the horses and the buggies and the other property. I pass this list every day and often I stop in front of it and just speak their name out loud and their ages, Jonas, 11 years old, $500. Sarah, 41 years old, $900. Elizabeth, 57, $800. I force myself to consider the absurdity and the obscenity of prices being a fixed to each one, should they be placed up for sale. I sometimes just pause before them with a prayer. Particularly before I have to make a big decision about one of my companies or whether I move forward or whether I stay still. It reminds me, speaking those names out loud, not only of where I've come from, but how far I have to go because of them.

It reminds me that I am never alone. It reminds me of what I've come through to get through. Even when I find myself in settings where I am the only black woman still, that kind of singularity, it doesn't make me uncomfortable. I got to tell you, it never has made me uncomfortable. I walk into a room just as cool as you please and to a man, the fellows tend to fall down on their knees. Because I've always known I was never anywhere God didn't want me to be. I've had no issues accepting the success or being worthy of what I know I work for. But these days it simply makes me wonder, though when I'm still the only woman or person of color sitting at the table, where my sisters are? It makes me wonder who has constructed what obstacles aimed at keeping them out. Because without artificial barriers, we would be represented in every room, where the criteria are excellence and discipline and determination and vision, we would be there at that table.

These moments when I walk into the room, just as cool as you please and I'm the only person of color, I'm the only woman. These are the moments I call upon the ancestors to surround me, to sustain me, to strengthen me. I call up on them here today, I call up on them and I offer myself to them, I say, I am here. I am ready and okay you all, here we go. Because when

OPRAH WINFREY

I walk into any room, when and where I enter, I am already more than I was. I already embody the truth of Maya Angelou's wise words when she said, "I come as one, but I stand as 10,000." I stand not only as 10,000, I stand as 10,000 to the tenth power. I stand on solid rock, I stand. I stand because I am the dream and the hope of the slave, and I am more than the seed of the free that Langston Hughes talked about the Negro mother. I am the fruit. I am the flower. I am the blossoming tree, and I shall not be moved. Ain't I a woman?

When I walk with them, when I walked with that 10,000, this is how I'm carried through life. I'm carried through life, standing with the 10,000. When I walk with them, I remember something else Maya taught me that Jimmy Baldwin taught her. She used to say to me, "Baby, your crown has been paid for. All you got to do is put it on your head and wear it." When we come into this museum, we get to see how the crowns were laid out for us. That's what you did for us, Lonnie Bunch, you laid the crowns out so we can see in plain view. We get to see and feel that sense of connection to the past, that allows us to step out of our history and step into a future that is brighter than any of them could've ever imagined.
But here we are now together, reshaping our history to finally reflect the truth, the whole truth and nothing but the truth. That's what this museum is all about and we're learning to understand and learning to embrace the power from which we have come. That power I'm telling you, that power, that

sense of spiritual energy that you feel here, that's the way station. It's the fuel tank, it's the mainstay of all empowerment. Look at what they did, now imagine what you can do. We need to wrap ourselves in Sojourner's certainty when we say yes, this is our story. Yes, you need to know that story. You need to know it in order to know yourself. You need to know it in order to know your strength and to understand that strength, times strength, equals power. Look at what they did, and then imagine what you can do, what we can do together and then let's get about the business of doing it.

Hear the words of Pearl Cleage, she says, "We know that we are walking in the footprints, made deep by the confident strides of women who parted the air before them, like the forces of nature that they were." We are grateful because we need their wisdom now, we need it now more than ever. We need their clarity, and we need their courage, we need their vision to dream bigger. To climb higher, to sing louder, to walk taller, to be better. To allow ourselves to move around fearlessly in spaces that are big enough to hold all that we are. All that we have been and all that we are intended to be. The reason why so many of us can't move forward is that you're in a space too cramped to hold your spirit. You all cramped up.
You've got to be in alignment with what it is you want to do, otherwise the empowerment doesn't work. We have got to stay ready, we've got to stay tuned up spiritually. Starts in here and moves outward. We've got to stay tuned up spiritually, mentally, so that when we are asked to create

whole worlds from scratch, we say yes! Yes! of course, we can. Because that creating thing, that's our specialty, that's what we do. We have so many worlds inside of us, so many starlet galaxies, so many deep rivers of wisdom and so much truth. We know so much, and we have so much joy, so much joy buried, waiting, bursting to get out. Yes, we'll be happy to share them, we are just waiting. We've been waiting on y'all to see it and to ask.

Because we've always known the answer to Sojourner's question, ain't I a woman? The answer is yes. Always and forever yes, I am a woman in full, fully grown whole. A phenomenal woman as Maya said and when you see me walk in, it ought to make you proud. Hear the words of Mari Evans, "I am a black woman. The music of my song, some sweet arpeggio of tears is written in a minor key, and I can be heard. Humming in the night. I can be heard humming in the night because I'm a black woman. Tall as a Cyprus. I'm a black woman strong. Beyond all definition, still they keep trying, but beyond definition, still define place I am. Define time, I am and circumstance. I am a black woman. Assailed? Yes. Impervious? Yes. Indestructible? Yes. I am a black woman, look upon me and be renewed. Thank you.
I said to Lonnie, I love taking questions. I love the spirit and energy of this place. So, I'm happy to take questions for as long as they tell me I can. It was so fun, remember, I told you walking into the exhibit yesterday and the Mari Evans book is

there, and I said, I'm going to do that. It's one of my favorite poems. Anybody got a question?

Audience Member: What inspires you every single day? Because you inspire us every moment anytime we see you. What inspires you?

Oprah: I will tell you, I live in the space of inspiration for myself, and I thank you for saying that. The truth is, my calling is to inspire, and I have been doing that since I was three years old in the Kosciusko, Methodist Buffalo Church, that you'll see when you see the exhibit. That's where I started out doing Easter pieces. Jesus rose on Easter day, hallelu, hallelu, all the angels proclaim. You know in the black culture, we would get all the old hymnals that had been passed down from the white churches. We'd get all their discarded stuff, so you would just get like a little piece of a thing, and they'd hand it to you, and they'd say, this is your piece to learn for either Mother's Day or Easter or Christmas. So, my broadcasting career actually started in the church doing those pieces.

I recognize that the thread of my purpose in life began there. Just like yours, if you start thinking about where did your yearning to be you start? For me, it started in the church, with the sisters in the front row fanning themselves, saying to my grandmother, "Hattie Mae, this is a talking child." I went through the whole exhibit, it's quite extraordinary. When I say hashtag goals to have your exhibit on exhibit at a museum. But I got through the whole exhibit yesterday, and the thing that made me cry was at the end, there was a book where people had written just what the exhibit meant to them and what the Oprah Show had meant to them over the years. A woman wrote, "Watching you every day is the reason why I love myself so fiercely." That made me cry, because that is my goal, my intention is to use my life as an inspiration to other people, to see what is possible for themselves.

Not my life is impossible, but my life is an inspiration for you to see the light in your own. What makes me the happiest is when somebody gets that, and all the years on the Oprah show, I could always feel when I had connected to the audience. When something was said, and it was actually heard and people liked. I remember the time I shared something that Maya had taught me about when people show you who they are, believe them. I could feel people get it. I could feel people get it because the people in the audience, they just did what you just did, "mmhm yes."

Then somebody said, you teach people how to treat you and people go, "mhmm yes." You can feel when you're connecting and you're doing that. There is nothing that makes me happier in life than making other people be able to fulfill their own happiness. I have all these beautiful girls who are some of them, I thought I saw you ask a question. But beautiful girls from South Africa, hello, stand-up girls, so they can see you. All these girls I've known since they were 12, 13 years old. Now they're all graduating college and going out into the world. I tell them all the time, don't worry about a mother's day gift, don't worry about that. First of all, words are important, so knowing how you feel is important. But the other thing is your happiness is my reward. Your success is my reward. My only goal is to have opened the door and you being smart enough, wise enough to step through that door and accept the opportunity. What inspires me is having other people be inspired. Thank you. Yes. Ma'am. I can hear you.

Audience Member: Hi, I am a young black female from Baltimore. You got your start in Baltimore, a lot of people ask me about my journey so far, sometimes they'd say how could that happen to you? I believe in the power of manifestation.

Oprah: It's true

Audience Member: I want you to speak with everyone about the power of meditation and manifestation and how.

Oprah: Thank you for that and good luck with your career. Yes, you're a manifestor so that's good. I'm a big manifester, but here's the deal. There is no dream that you can dream that the power that is God, regardless of what name you call it, has not dreamed bigger for you. Let's just for the sake of everybody be on the same page, let's use life for God. Life has dreamed a dream for you and your goal, your number one job is to figure out what that dream is and align yourself with the dream. Because the dream cannot come to you unless you're willing to meet it energetically in the same place. If your energy is off, which I say to my girls all the time, they could teach this class right now, on being in flow. If you are not in flow with God's dream for you, with life's dream for you. If you are out of order, if you are out of sync, it cannot come to you. It will not come, because the whole purpose of your life is to line yourself up with the purpose.

If you are operating in fear, if you are operating in jealousy, jealousy will kill you. Any kind of anger or jealousy you have about anybody else. So here are a couple of laws I have, the first law is the third law of motion in physics, which says for every action, there's an equal and opposite reaction. We showed that very beautifully in The Color Purple, when Ms. Sealey says to Mister, "Everything you even try to do to me is already done to you." That is not just a rhetorical saying that is law. That is Newton's third law of motion in physics, which says everything that goes out is coming back. It's just like everything that goes up is coming down, it may take it a long time to come down, it's coming down. Everything that goes out is coming back, it's coming back. To answer the power of manifestation and meditation, what meditation does is sync you up with the source.
What meditation does is allows you to literally tap into the power that created you, so that you are in alignment with that. So, when you carry that out into the world, everything that you do comes from the center of that alignment, that's coming from the source that we call God. We call it divine energy, divine intelligence, whatever name you want to give it to, we call it life. When you are synced up with life, life just

gives to you. It opens doors, it creates experiences. It allows you to meet people. Things show up you never thought were going to show up. You are doing, what is the purpose of your soul being here. One of my favorite teachers is Gary Zuckav who says that "Authentic power is when you learn to use your personality," which I've done very well. "Use your personality to serve the energy of your soul."

You are the bigger soul that has a personality. When you figure out how to take, I have a big personality. It's lovely, it's charming, but it's not me. I'm here to do my soul's work and I use my personality to serve the soul's work and because I know what the soul's work is. I heard somebody ask earlier about what should you be praying. The prayer is using me. You are here to be used as a vessel from the source, from which you have come. Everybody has a different talent and the reason we're all so messed up is because you're looking at everybody else's talent and wishing you had some of their talent. All the energy that you spend thinking about, wishing about, being jealous of, envious of anybody else is energy that you're not only putting out, it's going to come back to you negatively. But you're taking that away from you, all your energy should be forced on what do I have to offer? What do I have to give? How can I be used in service?

Because Dr. King's message of not everybody can be famous, but everybody can be great because greatness is determined by service. There is not a job in here that you can do that you don't switch the paradigm to service and not make that job more fulfilling. I don't care what the job is, if you say I'm a singer, I'm a dancer, I'm an artist. I'm a teacher, I'm a nurse. I'm a doctor, I'm a janitor, I'm a clerk. If you say, if I look at this from, how do I use this in service to something bigger than myself? It no longer becomes a job. It becomes an offering to the world and that is why you're here. When you can line up with whatever that is, line up with that, and all you have to do is keep asking the question and ask the question in purity, not in when it is going to come? You know like I'm not looking for a man, but is that him over there?

I played that game. When you could do that, then it comes, it opens up, don't you see that? Don't you see the difference between the days you meditate, and you don't? Yes, I try to do it every day, cause if you don't, it's usually a more messed up day. Doesn't mean you don't get through life, cause a lot of people getting through life, it just means your life isn't as enhanced. Everybody who's afraid of meditation, don't even call it meditation. Don't call it that, just say, I have a prayer chair, I have just a place where it's going to be still. The Bible says, be still and know, because that's the only way you can know. That's the only knowing. You actually do already know there's nothing you don't know and that's why an aha moment is an aha. Because an aha is a remembering of what you already know.

Somebody says something, you're in church, the preacher says something you already knew that. It's just reminding you, it's reminding you that you have forgotten who you were and where you came from. There is nothing that you cannot do if it is not aligned with the greater source. The reason why people have so many struggles is because you're struggling against what is for you. You're pushing against it, so when you find that you're not moving forward, you need to stop and get still and say, what am I resisting? What am I pushing against? Because it can't come through if you push against it. It only comes through if you're in flow with it and it just flows, it flows and it cannot flow if you're afraid.

Audience Member: My name is Shawn Renee. We do live storytelling, there are pop-up events all over the country. We bring in groups of women together to tell stories about a central thing. I curated the show, I bring them all together and we rehearse the shows through workshops or stories, and there are some very important stories that need to be taught. But they're very nervous when I put them in front of the non-black audience. They could do it here, but when I take them outside, I don't know, I'm afraid that they don't quite understand.

Oprah: Well, I think that's because there's still some shame stuff involved. There's like, nobody will understand. I'm going to go around the way to answer that question. I have this girl's school in South Africa, and I started it with the idea of taking girls who've come from challenged environments and bringing them into the school and giving them this great opportunity. Which all of that's working because every one of my girls is brilliant. Even the small rural schools that they come from, we went around Gayle and I the first year, handpicking every single girl. So, every girl you see here today has been handpicked because they were smart wherever they were.

Then they come into my school, and they're all thrown off because everybody's smart. It's the first time they've ever been in a place and that's their first breakdown, oh Lord, I would be number one, now I'm number 12, Mamo. One of the things that has absolutely helped to turn my school around is the opening up and sharing of stories. That started because Mpumi started doing it, speaking around the country and sharing her story.

Audience Member: Wow, I just love sharing stories, I was open to it when I was nine years old and decided to enjoy it. I just knew that when I told the story, I could see more myself and my root, and somehow, it's worth watching and now it's a movement for South Africa.

Oprah: But at first though, you were afraid to share the story. All the girls, over half of our girls have lost their parents, both parents to AIDS in my school. Everybody was ashamed of telling the story because they thought they were the only one, right?

Audience Member: Yes.

Oprah: Now, you know, that there's nothing you can share. So thanks Pums. But I would say this, the reason why I was number one for 25 years is because I figured out early on, there is no story anybody has ever heard that somebody else hasn't experienced. Nothing. I also figured out, probably maybe the first or second year, that all pain is the same. That a mother in Somalia feels the same way as a mother in Seattle when she loses her child. The common denominator in the human experience is our emotions and our feelings. The more vulnerable and open you are willing to be with your story, the more actual understanding you create with other people and the more powerful you become. People don't think less of you for sharing your story. They think more of you for having the courage to share it.

So that's what I would say to your women, there is nothing that they can say that hasn't been felt. The classic example of this was when I did Toni Morrison for the first time on the book club or a second time, I chose Bluest Eye. Now Bluest Eye is, intrinsically a black story about a little black girl who wants to have blue eyes, because she doesn't know enough about herself or doesn't think she's beautiful. I thought this was going to be a story that black women all over the world would relate to. Women in Brazil, women in the Philippines, women in Korea, women in China, women all over the world said I am that girl. I was actually surprised at like, how is everybody that girl? Because everybody has experienced that feeling of being the outcast because you didn't look like everybody else thought you were supposed to look.

Another great example was when I went to interview in the mid to late eighties, a group of women in prison in Texas, all accused of killing their children and there were six of them. All murderers in for life and I sat around with them, spent an afternoon with them. Ate with them, talk with them and at the end, one of them came up and said, you're the first person who's ever treated us like we were real people. How could you sit with us because you know we've done terrible things? I said, because I realized in talking to you, that all pain is the same and this is what you did with yours. So there is no story, all stories have the basic seven themes of pain or suffering or loss or triumph or whatever.

When you get to the core of what's really going on, everybody who's lost a mother. It's why when Ava DuVernay had this beautiful scene, anybody watch Queen Sugar in here? First season, you see the first episode or second episode when the father dies. The three generations, the father is on the bed dying, Ralph Angel is there with his younger son. It's why people all over the world cried because everybody knows what it's like. Anybody who's ever been in a hospital room and had to have that moment. It knows no color, it knows no background. It knows no creed, no belief system. So, when you get to the root of what's really happening, we all feel the same. That is why I was able to be so successful, because I knew that we started in Chicago, and I was on the air for a year in Chicago, Look at that exhibit, we were looking at me on the first day, I am actually wearing white stockings. I did not go to nurse's school, I am wearing white stockings with a Jerry curl with a skirt too long and a coat too short. Nobody, but Jesus could have helped me at that particular time.

Gayle just said to me yesterday, no way you could've made it today. No way you could have made it. But I understood that there was a common denominator in the human experience, because we had already been talking to all these women in Chicago for years and their feelings and their emotions and what they'd been through. I know that just because you are across the state line in Iowa, you're not going to feel any different. Or because you're in Michigan, you're not going to feel any different because you're in Ohio because you're in Seattle because you're in Boston, you don't feel any different, it's all the same. Everybody who's been cheated on feels the same. No matter what color you are, you feel the same. You're mad! You're mad.

Audience Member: Hi I'm Brittany and I am in a place of deep gratitude and confirmation. I want to ask you about calling. I was one of those folks who struggled because I was running from mine. Finally decided that I wanted to get in alignment and discovered in just the past few weeks that my calling is very simply to speak truth. Two days after I discovered that, I got the invitation to be on stage here.

Oprah: That's what I mean. That's the way it happens.

Audience Member: As I walked through the exhibit, before this portion, I read the journal entry that you wrote midnight before the airing of your first national show, where you said maybe this is my calling. I would love to know from you, what took you from the place of maybe to assuredness and your calling and keeps you in the place of being unafraid and unapologetic about exactly what it is.

Oprah: Great question. Well, what took me from maybe to a certainty was actually a show I did with the Ku Klux Klan. That's why if I leave you with nothing else, just know this for sure. There is not one thing that has ever happened to you. Not one experience, not one encounter, not one crisis, not one joyful thing that hasn't happened just to make you better and help you rise. Every single thing you're calling in whether you know it or not. When you figure out that you are calling it in, when you actually start meditating or praying or doing, or having a spiritual practice, which is the number one thing you need, if you want to be successful in the world. You need something that gives back and nourishes you, regardless of what you call that. You need to, you need to fill your cup so that you can be so full your cup runneth over, and you have enough to give to other people.

If you don't fill your cup, you end up dried up. You end up tired, exhausted, and don't have enough to give to other people. You end up resentful every time somebody asks you because your cup is empty and now, they want some of yours.

So, your number one job is to fill your cup and make yourself whole. That's your job.
I was happy to just be on TV. I've been on TV since I was 19. I met my best friend Gayle in Baltimore. I knew that that wasn't my calling, being a television reporter. I hated it, she loves it. I always felt out of alignment with myself, but my father was like, "Girl don't give up that job." "You are making $25,000 a year and you're 25, don't give up that job."

I had those voices, but every day I was, I wouldn't say agony, I was trying to find how can I be myself, be real on the air? I always felt like I was pretending and that I was out of alignment. Then, when they got ready to fire me, they were going to fire me. But they didn't want to release me from the contract, so they thought, well, let's just pay her out and we can get her to do this talk show thing. So, they literally put me on the talk show to get me out of the way and the very first day I sat there interviewing the Carvel ice-cream man about his multiple flavors and Benny from All My Children. Remember? Benny used to be on All my Children. Those are my two first guests and doing dollar for dollars in between, I knew that I had come home to myself. I could not predict that it would turn into what it has, but I knew that I could finally breathe. I was no longer pretending to restrict my feelings because I go out on stories, and I would empathize with people. I feel bad for them and that would show up in the work.

Then I would get a little slip from my boss, cause I had a really aggressive, bad boss. I started to feel then, oh this is the job that I want, but I didn't know about calling. I was interviewing a woman on one of the shows, it was so impressive for me to see all the shows that we've done. Lord, make me tired looking at it. But I was interviewing a woman, it was a show called the Wives Meet the Mistresses or some crazy thing. This woman was on, and it was a live show and in the middle of it, her husband tells the wife and our entire audience and the world that his mistress was pregnant. Yes, to this day, it makes my eyes water because I saw his wife's face and I felt her humiliation. I said I will quit TV if I have to do this, I won't do this anymore. My producers like, what are we going to do? This is what everybody's doing. Then during that same time period, I said, I'm not going to do anything like that anymore. I'm not going to bring people on TV.

First of all, we didn't know that moment was going to happen. They were like, we didn't know it was going to happen. But that should not happen on television, and I do not want to be a part of the energy that caused somebody to feel that, because that's not going to come back to me, I got to pay for that. Then I was interviewing the KKK on stage, that was the day the one guy called me a monkey in the audience. During commercial break, I could see them signaling each other and just watching them and their behavior I thought, oh, they get it. I don't get it. They are using me, they're using this platform because they understand. Cause I'm thinking, oh, I'm going to tell you all about the KKK. They were using it to recruit members for themselves. They were using it to recruit their base. I then went to the producers and said not doing a show like that. So, they said, you're not going to do the mistresses, you're not going to do the KKK, what are we going to do?

I said, we are going to create a baseline for ourselves that's based on intention. This was around 1989 when I'd read Gary Zukav's book called The Seat of the Soul. That book was life-changing for me, because in it he talked about the power of intention and cause and effect, what goes out, comes back and is determined by your intention. The energy of your intention is what determines your life. Most people don't think about their intention, they just think about what they want to do. Most people don't think about why they want to do it, but what's going to come back to you, the energy that's going to come back to you is the real why of why you did it. I then said to my producers, we're not going to do any shows that are not intentional. So, don't bring me an idea unless you have an intention for the show that you want the outcome to be. We're going to strive to see if we can live up to our intentions.

Around the late eighties, we started a pre-show to talk about what the intention was and then a post-show after every single show to say, did we fulfill that intention? That's about the time I realized this is bigger than me and my journal prayers, if you were to look at my journal over the years, is that I started to recognize that it wasn't just a show and the KKK helped me to see that. It wasn't a show, it was a platform to be used as a mission, just like they were recruiting their base. I could recruit mine and I was going to recruit for good. I said to the producers, we're going to be a force for good, we're going to use this to inspire your question. We're going to use this to uplift wherever we can and we're going to use it to inspire, uplift, encourage and entertain. Your show ideas have to include some little bit of all of that. Did it inspire somebody? Uplift somebody? Did it encourage somebody? Did you also do that in a way that was entertaining?

You will know it's your calling when you would do it for nothing. You will know that you're in alignment. I mean our team worked 14, 18-hour days every single day. Then we take three months off and then come back and try to do better. We were our own competition. The only competition.

OPRAH WINFREY

Powerful Eulogy for Toni Morrison
(2019)

Good evening. I must say that I've been speaking since I was three years old in churches. I'm never nervous or intimidated, but writers are rock stars to me. So to have this entire row of rock stars, I'm shaking inside, I feel so honored to be in your presence. And thank you, Errol McDonald for inviting me to be here today.

The first time I came face to face with Toni Morrison was in Maya Angelou's backyard for a gathering of some of the most illustrious black people you've ever heard of, to celebrate Toni Morrison's Nobel Prize victory. My head and my heart were swirling. Every time I looked at her, I couldn't even speak. I had to catch my breath. I was seated across from her at dinner, and there was a moment when I saw Ms. Morrison just gesture to the waiter for some water, and I almost tripped over myself trying to get up from the table to get it for her. And Maya said, "Sit down. We have people here to do that. You're a guest." So I sat down, I obeyed of course. But it was not easy, I tell you, to sit still or to keep myself inside my body. I felt like I was all of seven years old. Cause after all, she was there, and so many others, that day. Mari Evans, Sister Angela Davis was there, Nikki Giovanni was there, Rita Dove was there.... It was a writer's mecca. And I was there, sitting at the table, taking it all in. As I look back, that day remains one of the great thrills of my life.

You know, I didn't really get to speak to Toni Morrison that day. I was just too bedazzled. But I had already previously called her up to ask about acquiring the film rights to *Beloved*. After I finished reading it, I found her number, called her, and when I asked her, is it true that sometimes people have to read over your work in order to understand it, to get the full meaning? She bluntly replied, "That, my dear, is called reading." I was embarrassed but that statement actually gave me the confidence years later when I formed a book club on The Oprah Show to choose her work. I chose more of her books than any other author over the years. *Song of Solomon,* First, *Sula, The Bluest Eye,* and *Paradise.* And if any one of our viewers complained that it was hard going or challenging, reading Toni Morrison, I simply said: "That, my dear, is called reading."

There was no distance between Toni Morrison and her words. I loved her novels but lately I've been re-reading her essays, which underscore that she was also one of our most influential public intellectuals. In one essay, she said: "If writing is thinking and discovering and selection and order and meaning, it is also awe and reverence and mystery and magic." And this: "Facts can exist without human intelligence, but truth cannot." She thought deeply about the role of the artist and concluded that writers are among the most sensitive, the most intellectually anarchic, most representative, most probing of all the artists. She believed it was a writer's job to rip the veil off to bore down to the truth. She took the canon, she broke it open.

OPRAH WINFREY

Among her legacies were writers she paved the way for, many of them here, in this beautiful space tonight, celebrating her. Toni Morrison was her words, she is her words, for her words often were confrontational. She spoke the unspoken, she probed the unexplored. She wrote of eliminating the white gaze, of not wanting to speak for black people, but wanting to speak to them. To be among them. To be among all people. Her words don't permit the reader to down them quickly and forget them, we know that. They refuse to be skimmed. They will not be ignored. They can gut you, turn you upside down, make you think you just don't get it. But when you finally do, when you finally do and you always will, when you open yourself to what she is offering, you experience, as I have many times reading Toni Morrison, a kind of emancipation. A liberation, an ascension to another level of understanding. Because by taking us down there, amid the pain, the shadows, she urges us to keep going, to keep feeling, to keep trying to figure it all out, with her words and her stories as guide and companion.

She asks us to follow our own pain, to reckon with it, and at last, transcend it. While she's no longer on this earth, her magnificent soul, her boundless imagination, her fierce passion, her gallantry... she told me once, "I've always known I was gallant." Who says that? Who even knows they are gallant? Well, her gallantry remains always to help us navigate our way through. I'd like to close the evening with an excerpt. You know, I have many favorite passages when it comes to Toni's body of work... but this one, from *Song of Solomon,* never fails to inspire awe in me. And for that, and so much else, I say thank you to the singular, monumental, gallant writer.

"He had come out of nowhere, as ignorant as a hammer and broke as a convict, with nothing but free papers, a Bible, and a pretty black-haired wife, and in one year he'd leased ten acres, the next ten more. Sixteen years later he had one of the best farms in Montour County. A farm that colored their lives like a paintbrush and spoke to them like a sermon. 'You see?' the farm said to them. 'See? See what you can do? Never mind you can't tell one letter from another, never mind you born a slave, never mind you lose your name, never mind your daddy dead, never mind nothing. Here, this here, is what a man can do if he puts his mind to it and his back in it. Stop sniveling,' it said. 'Stop picking around the edges of the world.

Take advantage, and if you can't take advantage, take disadvantage. We live here. On this planet, in this nation, in this country right here. *No*where else! We got a home in this rock, don't you see! Nobody starving in my home; nobody crying in my home, and if I got a home you got one too! Grab it. Grab this land! Take it, hold it, my brothers, make it, my brothers, shake it, squeeze it, turn it, twist it, beat it, kick it, kiss it, whip it, stomp it, dig it, plow it, seed it, reap it, rent it, buy it, sell it, own it, build it, multiply it, and pass it on — can you hear me? Pass it on!'"

OPRAH WINFREY

Graduation Class of 2020 Commencement Speech

"I know you may not feel like it, but you are indeed the chosen class, for such a time as this...the class of 2020. You are also a united class—the pandemic class that has the entire world striving to graduate with you.

Of course this is not the graduation ceremony you envisioned: You've been dreaming about the walk across the stage, your family and friends cheering you on, the caps flung joyously in the air. But even though there may not be pomp because of our circumstances, never has a graduating class been called to step into the future with more purpose, vision, passion and energy, and hope.

Your graduation ceremony is taking place with so many luminaries celebrating you on the world's Facebook stage. I am just honored to join them and salute you.

The word graduate comes from the Latin gradus, meaning "a step toward something." In the early 15th century, "graduation" was a term used in alchemy to mean "a tempering or refining." Every one of us is now being called to graduate, to step toward something—even though we don't know what! Every one of us is likewise now being called to temper the parts of ourselves that must fall away, to refine who we are, how we define success, and what is genuinely meaningful. And you--the real graduates on this day: you will lead us.

I wish I could tell you I know the path forward. I don't. There is so much uncertainty. In truth, there always has been. What I do know is that the same values, fortitude, and determination (and I know you're determined, that's why we're celebrating your diplomas today)….the same guts and imagination that got you to this moment—all those things are the very things that will sustain you through whatever is coming.

It's vital that you learn, and we all learn, to be at peace with the discomfort of stepping into the unknown. It's really okay to not have all the answers. The answers will come—for sure—if you can accept, "not knowing" long enough to get still, and stay still long enough for new thoughts to take root in your more quiet, deeper, truer self. The noise of the world drowns out the sound of you; you have to get still to listen.

So can you use this disorder that COVID-19 has wrought? Can you treat it as an uninvited guest that's come into our midst to reorder our way of being? Can you, the class of 2020, show us not how to put the pieces back together again, but how to create a new and more evolved normal, a world more just, kind, beautiful, tender, luminous, creative, whole?

We need you to do this because the pandemic has illuminated the vast systemic inequities that have defined life for too many for too long. For poor communities without adequate access to healthcare, inequality is a pre-existing condition. For immigrant communities forced to hide in the shadows, inequality is a pre-existing condition. For incarcerated people with no ability to social distance, inequality is a pre-existing condition. For every person burdened by bias and bigotry, for every black man and woman living in their American skin, fearful to even go for a jog, inequality is a pre-existing condition.

You have the power to stand for, to fight for—and vote for—healthier conditions that will create a healthier society. This moment is your invitation to use your education to begin to heal our afflictions, by applying the best of what you've learned in your head and felt in your heart.

This moment has shown us what Dr. King tried to tell us. Decades ago he understood that "we are caught in an inescapable network of mutuality, tied into a single garment of destiny." That's what he said. "Whatever affects one directly, affects all indirectly."

If humanity is a global body, every soul is a cell in that body. And we are being challenged as never before to keep the global body healthy by keeping ourselves healthy in mind, body and spirit. As all the traditions affirm, the deepest self-care is at once caring for the human family.

We see this so clearly with essential workers. Look who turns out to be essential! Teachers—your teachers!—healthcare workers of course, the people stocking grocery shelves, the cashiers, the truck drivers, food providers, those who are caring for your grandparents, those who clean the places where we work and shop and carry out our daily lives. We are all here because they, at great and profound risk, are still providing their essential service.

What will *your* essential service be?

What really matters to you? The fact that you're alive means you've been given a reprieve to think deeply about that question. How will you use what matters in service to yourself, your community, and the world? For me it has always been talking and sharing stories. For you—well, that's for you to discover.

My hope is that you will harness your education, your creativity, your valor, your voice, your vote—reflecting on all that you've witnessed and hungered for, all that you know to be true—and use it to create more equity, more justice, and more joy in the world.

To be the class that COMMENCED a new way forward. The class of 2020. Bravo. Brava brava Brava."

Oprah Announcing the Coming End of her Show
(2009)

So at the top of the show, I told you that I have some news to share with you.

So here goes after much prayer and months of careful thought. I've decided that next season, season 25 will be the last season of the Oprah Winfrey Show.

And over the next couple of days, you may hear a lot of speculation in the press about why I am making this decision now, and that will mostly be conjecture.

So, I wanted you to hear this directly from me.

Twenty-four years ago, on September 8, 1986, I went live from Chicago to launch the first national Oprah Winfrey Show.

I was beyond excited. And as you all might expect, a little nervous, I knew then what a miraculous opportunity I had been given.

But I certainly never could have imagined the yellow brick road of blessings that have led me to this moment with you. These years with you our viewers have enriched my life beyond all measure.

And you all have graciously invited me into your living rooms into your kitchens and into your lives.

And for some of you long time, Oprah viewers, you have literally grown up with me. We've grown together.

You had your families and you raise your children and you left a spot for me in your morning or your afternoon, depending on when the Oprah Show airs in your town.

So, I just wanted to say that whether you've been here with me from the beginning or you came on board last week, I want you all to know that my relationship with you is one that I hold very dear and your trust in me, the sharing of your precious time every day with me has brought me the greatest joy I have ever known. So here we are, halfway through the season 24, and it still means as much to me to spend an hour every day with you as it did back in 1986.

So why walk away and make next season the last here is the real reason I love this show.

This show has been my life and I love it enough to know when it's time to say goodbye. Twenty-five years feels right in my bones and it feels right in my spirit. It's the perfect number, the exact right time.

I hope that you will take this 18-month ride with me right through to the final show over this holiday break my team and I will be brainstorming new ways that we can entertain you, inform you and uplift you when we return here in January. And then season 25, we are going to knock your socks off.

So, the countdown to the end of the Oprah Winfrey Show starts now, and until that day in 2011, when it ends, I intend to soak up every meaningful, joyful moment with you.

Thanks everybody, and I'll see you.

OPRAH WINFREY

Final Words on the last Oprah Winfrey's Show
(2011)

Every single day I came down from my makeup room on our harpo elevator, I would offer a prayer of gratitude for the delight and the privilege of doing this show.
Gratitude is the single greatest treasure I will take with me from this experience. The opportunity to have done this work to be embraced by all of you who watched is one of the greatest honors a human being could have.

I've been asked many times during this farewell season, is ending the show bittersweet? Well, I say all sweet, no bitter. And here's why, many of us have been together for 25 years. We have hooted and hollered together, had our aha moments, we ugly cried together and we did our gratitude journals.

So I thank you all for your support and your trust in me. I thank you for sharing this yellow brick road of blessings.
I thank you for tuning in every day along with your mothers and your sisters and your daughters, your partners gay and otherwise, your friends and all the husbands who got coaxed into watching Oprah. I thank you for being as much of a sweet inspiration for me as I've tried to be for you.

I won't say goodbye. I'll just say, until we meet again.
To God be the glory.

Oprah Winfrey's Quotes

Where there is no struggle there is no strength.

It doesn't matter who you are, where you come from. The ability to triumph begins with you – always.

Forgiveness is letting go of the hope that the past can be changed.

I would like to thank the people who've brought me those dark moments, when I felt most wounded, betrayed. You have been my greatest teachers.

The great courageous act that we must all do, is to have the courage to step out of our history and past so that we can live our dreams.

Turn your wounds into wisdom.

You look at yourself and you accept yourself for who you are, and once you accept yourself for who you are you become a better person.

If you want your life to be more rewarding, you have to change the way you think.

In the mist of Difficulty lies Opportunity.

Doing the best at this moment puts you in the best place for the next moment.

Do the one thing you think you cannot do. Fail at it. Try again. Do better the second time. The only people who never tumble are those who never mount the high wire. This is your moment. Own it.

I know for sure that what we dwell on is who we become.

Wherever you are in your journey, I hope you, too, will keep encountering challenges. It is a blessing to be able to survive them, to be able to keep putting one foot in front of the other—to be in a position to make the climb up life's mountain, knowing that the summit still lies ahead. And every experience is a valuable teacher.

Every time you suppress some part of yourself or allow others to play you small, you are ignoring the owner's manual your Creator gave you. What I know for sure is this: You are built not to shrink down to less but to blossom into more. To be more splendid. To be more extraordinary. To use every moment to fill yourself up.

One of the hardest things in life to learn are which bridges to cross and which bridges to burn.

You can have it all. Just not all at once.

It makes no difference how many peaks you reach if there was no pleasure in the climb.

When people show you who they are ... believe them!

OPRAH WINFREY

You get to know who you really are in a crisis.

If friends disappoint you over and over, that's in large part your own fault. Once someone has shown a tendency to be self-centered, you need to recognize that and take care of yourself; people aren't going to change simply because you want them to.

True forgiveness is when you can say, Thank you for that experience.

I trust that everything happens for a reason, even if we are not wise enough to see it.

I believe that every single event in life happens in an opportunity to choose love over fear.

I don't believe in failure. It's not failure if you enjoy the process.

Real integrity is doing the right thing, knowing that nobody's going to know whether you did it or not.

You are responsible for your life. You can't keep blaming somebody else for your dysfunction. Life is really about moving on.

So go ahead. Fall down. The world looks different from the ground.

It doesn't matter how far you might rise. At some point you are bound to stumble... If you're constantly pushing yourself higher, the law of averages, not to mention the Myth of Icarus, predicts that you will at some point fall. And when you do I want you to know this, remember this: there is no such thing as failure. Failure is just life trying to move us in another direction.

You've got to follow your passion. You've got to figure out what it is you love – who you really are. And have the courage to do that. I believe that the only courage anybody ever needs is the courage to follow your own dreams.

The key to realizing a dream is to focus not on success but significance, and then even the small steps and little victories along your path will take on greater meaning.

I have crossed over on the backs of Sojourner Truth, Harriet Tubman, Fannie Lou Hamer, and Madam C. J. Walker. Because of them I can now live the dream. I am the seed of the free, and I know it. I intend to bear great fruit.

All of us need a vision for our lives, and even as we work to achieve that vision, we must surrender to the power that is greater than we know. It's one of the defining principles of my life that I love to share: God can dream a bigger dream for you than you could ever dream for yourself.

The more you praise and celebrate your life, the more there is in life to celebrate.'

The way to choose happiness is to follow what is right and real and the truth for you. You can never be happy living someone else's dream. Live your own. And you will for sure know the meaning of happiness.

Bravery shows up in everyday life when people have the courage to live their truth, their vision and their dreams.

Whatever our dreams, ideas, or projects, we plant a seed, nurture it — and then reap the fruits of our labors.

I urge you to pursue preserving your personal history to allow your children and grandchildren to know who you were as a child and what your hopes and dreams were.

Your calling isn't something that somebody can tell you about. It's what you feel. It is the thing that gives you juice. The thing that you are supposed to do. And nobody can tell you what that is. You know it inside yourself.

The best thing about dreams is that fleeting moment, when you are between asleep and awake, when you don't know the difference between reality and fantasy, when for just that one moment you feel with your entire soul that the dream is reality, and it really happened.

I've come to believe that each of us has a personal calling that's as unique as a fingerprint – and that the best way to succeed is to discover what you love and then find a way to offer it to others in the form of service, working hard, and also allowing the energy of the universe to lead you.

Don't worry about being successful, but work toward being significant and the success will naturally follow.

The biggest adventure you can ever take is to live the life of your dreams.

Listen to the rhythm of your own calling, and follow that.

Anything you can imagine you can create.

The reason I've been able to be so financially successful is my focus has never, ever for one minute been money.

Cheers to a new year and another chance for us to get it right.

Your true passion should feel like breathing; it's that natural.

As you become more clear about who you really are, you'll be better able to decide what is best for you – the first time around.

When I look at the future, it's so bright it burns my eyes!

You have to find what sparks a light in you so that you in your own way can illuminate the world.

Challenges are gifts that force us to search for a new center of gravity. Don't fight them. Just find a new way to stand.

OPRAH WINFREY

Self-esteem comes from being able to define the world in your own terms and refusing to abide by the judgments of others.

To love yourself is a never-ending journey.

Leadership is about empathy. It is about having the ability to relate to and connect with people for the purpose of inspiring and empowering their lives.

The big secret in life is there is no secret. Whatever your goal. You can get there if you're willing to work.

I am grateful for the blessings of wealth, but it hasn't changed who I am. My feet are still on the ground. I'm just wearing better shoes.

Luck is a matter of preparation meeting opportunity.

With every experience, you alone are painting your own canvas, thought by thought, choice by choice.

Use your life to serve the world, and you will find that it also serves you.

Think like a queen. A queen if not afraid to fail. Failure is another stepping stone to greatness.

The more thankful I became, the more my bounty increased. That's because – for sure – what you focus on expands. When you focus on the goodness in life, you create more of it.

What I know is, is that if you do work that you love, and the work fulfills you, the rest will come.

I was once afraid of people saying, 'Who does she think she is?' Now I have the courage to stand and say, 'This is who I am.'

Passion is energy. Feel the power that comes from focusing on what excites you.

Breathe. Let go. And remind yourself that this very moment is the only one you know you have for sure.

This is a call to arms. A call to be gentle, to be forgiving, to be generous with yourself. The next time you look into the mirror, try to let go of the story line that says you're too fat or too sallow, too ashy or too old, your eyes are too small or your nose too big; just look into the mirror and see your face. When the criticism drops away, what you will see then is just you, without judgment, and that is the first step toward transforming your experience of the world.

Every day brings a chance for you to draw in a breath, kick off your shoes, and dance.

Everyone wants to ride with you in the limo, but what you want is someone who will take the bus with you when the limo breaks down.

OPRAH WINFREY

Some women have a weakness for shoes... I can go barefoot if necessary. I have a weakness for books.

Every day brings a chance to live free of regret and with as much joy, fun, and laughter as you can stand.

Follow your instincts. That's where true wisdom manifests itself.

Meditate. Breathe consciously. Listen. Pay attention. Treasure every moment. Make the connection.

The whole point of being alive is to evolve into the complete person you were intended to be.

Only make decisions that support your self-image, self-esteem, and self-worth.

Forgiveness is giving up the hope that the past could have been any different.

You are where you are in life because of what you believe is possible for yourself.

Surround yourself with only people who are going to lift you higher.

If a man wants you, nothing can keep him away. If he doesn't want you, nothing can make him stay.

Education is the key to unlocking the world, a passport to freedom.

Books were my pass to personal freedom. I learned to read at age three, and there discovered was a whole world to conquer that went beyond our farm in Mississippi.

Dogs are my favorite role models. I want to work like a dog, doing what I was born to do with joy and purpose. I want to play like a dog, with total, jolly abandon. I want to love like a dog, with unabashed devotion and complete lack of concern about what people do for a living, how much money they have, or how much they weigh. The fact that we still live with dogs, even when we don't have to herd or hunt our dinner, gives me hope for humans and canines alike.

I have a lot of things to prove to myself. One is that I can live my life fearlessly.

I don't want anyone who doesn't want me.

When you make loving others the story of your life, there's never a final chapter, because the legacy continues. You lend your light to one person, and he or she shines it on another and another and another. And I know for sure that in the final analysis of our lives- when the to-do lists are no more, when the frenzy is finished, when our e-mail inboxes are empty- the only thing that will have any lasting value is whether we've loved others and whether they've loved us.

OPRAH WINFREY

My idea of heaven is a great big baked potato and someone to share it with.

Even people who believe they deserve to be happy and have nice things often don't feel worthy once they have them.

Step out of the history that is holding you back. Step into the new story you are willing to create.

Live your life from truth and you will survive everything.

You will survive everything if you can live your life from the point of view of truth.

That took me a while to get, pretending to be something I wasn't, wanting to be somebody I couldn't, but understanding deep inside myself when I was willing to listen, that my own truth and only my own truth could set me free.

You will be wounded many times in your life. You'll make mistakes. Some people will call them failures but I have learned that failure is really God's way of saying, "Excuse me, you're moving in the wrong direction."

OPRAH WINFREY

Printed in Poland
by Amazon Fulfillment
Poland Sp. z o.o., Wrocław